CHIEFDOM:
THE WOMEN'S WORLD

SAMUEL ADENTWI BENTUM

Order this book online at www.trafford.com
or email orders@trafford.com

Most Trafford titles are also available at major online book retailers.

Printed in the United States of America.

ISB N: 978-1-4907-3940-3 (sc)
ISB N: 978-1-4907-3942-7 (hc)
ISB N: 978-1-4907-3941-0 (e)

Library of Congress Control Number: 2014910721

Publisher: Eric Kwadwo Amissah
Photographer: Ernest Doe Kudjordjie
Illustrator: Samuel Adentwi Bentum
Graphic Designer: Ernest Doe Kudjordjie
Cover Page Design: Ernest Doe Kudjordjie
English Language Editor: Sam-Ackah Odeyemi
Vernacular (Fanti) Editor: Elizabeth Prudence Yanney

Trafford rev. 06/16/2014

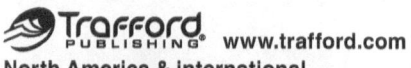 www.trafford.com
North America & international
toll-free: 1 888 232 4444 (USA & Canada)
fax: 812 355 4082

ACKNOWLEGEMENTS

My sincere thanks go to Mr. Sam-Ackah Odeyemi who read through the manuscript and made invaluable suggestions and also Eric Kwadwo Amissah who tactfully edited and co-ordinated the writing activity.

Ernest Doe Kudjordjie who took photographs of the carved pieces, designed and translated the manuscripts and photographs into a book.

My appreciation go to all those who helped me in one way or another; Bertha Mensah and Emma Ewusi Essoun for the careful and tactful typing of the manuscript. Ramos Asafo Agyei, Frederick N. Anderson and those who criticized, encouraged and moved the thoughts into this book, I appreciate all their efforts.

DEDICATION

To my niece, Phillipa Nketsiaba Benyah, who has great interest in my writing and artistry.

TABLE OF CONTENTS

LIST OF PLATES

LIST OF FIGURES

FOREWORD

In recent times, the knowledge in African culture has faded into oblivion. However, the cultural, intellectual and social richness of Africans vis-a-vis their civilization have direct relationship with the pulse of chiefdom.

It is therefore imperative that the young Africans be encouraged to acquire thorough knowledge in their culture in order to come to terms with their background, character, problems, ideals and way of life.

Dr. Bentum's use of women at the centre-stage of chiefdom in this book is fictional. He sees African women as strong forces to reckon with in social circles, therefore, they should be able to throw off the shackles of their past and assume higher responsibilities in chiefdom–this paints the dream of the emancipated woman who is empowered and shot to stardom.

In a nutshell, *Chiefdom: the Women's World* does not necessarily extol a smooth framework for African leadership, but depict a bright and clear account of how the chief and his elites in the Akan society function in concert to ensure effective administration.

SAM-ACKAH ODEYEMI
(Art critic, Prince, from Kikam Palace,
former Head, Liberal Studies Department,
former Dean, Student's Affairs,
Takoradi Polytechnic)

PREFACE

Chiefdom: the Women's World introduces a method of viewing and understanding art. For centuries, artists have relied on nature and tradition as their great sources of inspiration. Irregular wooden boards in their natural state are sculpturing resources that are worthy of adoration and adoption. Nature produces the images of Chiefdom on surfaces of wooden boards and by so doing, establishes the system of chiefdom.

The concept upon which these aesthetics and appreciations were figured out was based on the philosophy of truth which presents the materials, their sources and physical appearances as the basis of these sculptures. Therefore, the need to preserve and present the material was as crucial as the institution of chiefdom.

The style of presentation of these collections in this book centred on simplified realism that settled on plain geometric forms, shapes and lines. Carving technique was at times interspersed with the jagged shape of the wood boards, tree bark textures, surface perforations and marks from band and circular saws used in milling the timber into wooden boards. Titles of these relief sculptures were derived from the culture of Akan-Fante chiefdom and translated into English.

The females in these compositions are hyped to all the natural status of chiefdom even though some of the positions are the preserve of males. Hence, the dignity of the African culture in relation to Chiefdom is clearly and solidly sourced from the form and imagery produced from naturally shaped wood boards.

SAMUEL ADENTWI BENTUM
(Ph.D)

INTRODUCTION

Consider this book as an academic exercise which has evolved as a result of several thoughts, conversations and questions that revolved around the shape or form of irregular wooden boards. What information do these forms and features on the irregular wooden boards convey? In essence, they promote beautiful and interesting imagery which tends to capture the concept of Chiefdom. The prestige, reverence, authority and order associated with Chiefdom are vividly revealed on the surfaces of the wooden boards by nature. Nature, in this case directs the liberation of the images within these wooden boards and the philosophy of chiefdom.

Chiefdom, a form of hierarchical political organization in non-industrial societies, is usually based on kinship in which formal leadership is monopolized by the legitimate senior members of select families and elites. These elites form a political-ideological aristocracy relative to the general group. Chiefdom is thus led by a highly ranked incumbent of an inherited political role. Carneiro (1981: 45) defines chiefdom as *"an autonomous political unit comprising a number of villages or communities under the permanent control of a paramount chief".* In anthropological theory, one model of human social development rooted in ideas of cultural evolu-tion describes chiefdom as a form of social organization which is more complex than a tribe or a band society, and less complex than a state or a civilization. Carneiro (1981: 45) Chiefdoms are characterized by centralization of authority and pervasive inequality. At least two inherited social classes: the elites and the commoners are present – something that is common among Akans in ancient and modern Ghana.

In the vein of the philosophy of chiefdom on decentralization of authority and responsibility, this book outlines some aspects of the dignity associated with power and the service reposed in these elites in the administration of their king-

1

doms, towns and communities. These are revealed by the various shapes, forms and images that are on the surfaces of some irregular wooden boards. These relations provide a new identity that expresses the values of Akan Chiefdom and ethics that govern these kingdoms and communities. These natural designs become resources and commodities of aesthetics which coincide with the African philosophy of survival, growth and continuity. The irregular wooden boards were collected from saw mills, wood markets and furniture production factories and offered the needed attention and treatment that made them assume the new and seeming *real-life* features.

Nature and her attributes have for centuries acted as the major source of inspiration for artists. They provide the varied shapes, forms, textures and colours for artist to work with. Furthermore, the irregular wooden boards which would have otherwise been left to rot in the saw mills or the forest are used as raw materials for art production. Hence, the irregular boards become environment-friendly. It is therefore undeniable that nature as an inspirational vehicle connects generously with art. The individual wooden boards provide clues to the varied nature of chiefdom. Jagged edges, grooves, slots, and a lot more tend to motivate artists to produce compositions that relate to chiefdom – paramount chiefs, chiefs and sub-chiefs.

As a significant contribution to the world of art, this book seeks to deal with environmental cleaning in another dimension. Nature constantly inspires artists to undertake environmental cleaning through careful selection of irregular wooden boards as raw materials for art production. Like the adage "the stone the builders rejected has become the valuable stone" in this case the wooden board the wood factory rejected has become the precious material for wood carving. Although these irregular wooden boards are scientifically taken care of by nature as bio-degradable materials, their

constant presence on our environment creates a peril to mankind. Therefore, their identification and use as raw materials
for art production tend to organise the environment as well as
prevent it from becoming a danger to human beings and
animals.

What is Chiefdom?

It is a group of elites controlled by a single paramount centre, and ruled by a paramount chief. The paramount centre comprises of leaders of the elites. Established complex chiefdoms have two or even three tiers of political hierarchy – nobles, artisans or bureaucrats and commoners. Nobles are clearly distinct from commoners and do not usually engage in any form of agricultural or industrial production. The elites or higher members of society consume most of the goods that are produced for the hierarchy.

The ancient Hawaiian chiefdoms had as many as four social classes. An individual might change social class during a lifetime by extraordinary behaviour. A single lineage or family of the elite class becomes the ruling elites of the chiefdom who assume the greatest influence, power, and prestige. Chiefdom is typically a principle, while marriage, age, and sex can affect one's social status and role. Although commonly referred to as tribes, anthropologists classified their society as chiefdoms. They had a complex social hierarchy consisting of kings, warrior aristocracy, common freemen, serfs and slaves. (Carneiro: 1981)

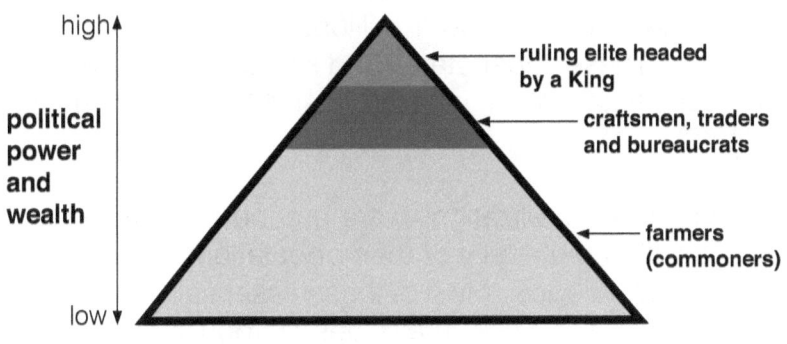

Pyramid of Power in Chiefdom
Courtesy: www.wikipedia.com

4

While centres of early civilization had major cultural and historical differences, they created remarkably similar political solutions for dealing with the problems of feeding and controlling large complex societies. These new political systems had a pyramid of authority with a small hereditary elite class at the top headed by a chief or a king and a royal family. At the bottom were the commoners who constituted the bulk of society. They were mostly the food producing farmers upon whom the entire society ultimately depended. In between the ruling elites and the commoners was a small middle class consisting of two groups. First, there were professional craftsmen and traders who mainly produced or acquired luxury items for the elites. Second, there were professional bureaucrats who administered the kingdom, town, village, community, religion and government on daily basis.

As independent kingdoms within each of the geographic regions of the ancient civilization, they competed for land, water, and other important resources and as a result, warfare became more frequent and larger in scale. Professional armies were created along with more efficient weapons such as metal swords, arrows, spear tips and guns. The consequence of these wars of conquest was the powerful kingdoms destroying and annexing the weaker ones. Eventually, the victors ruled enormous multi-city, multi-cultural, and multi-language empires with millions of people living over vast areas. These super-states and kingdoms required even more centralization of authority and larger permanent armies.

All of the ancient civilizations were pre-industrial agricultural societies with the majority of their populations living in hamlets and small villages. Most of these essentially rural societies only had one or a few small cities of about 5,000 - 50,000 people. These urban areas were primarily centres for the elite ruling class along with the state government bureaucracy and the majority of the full-time craft specialists and traders who worked for them. In addition, cities were the locations of major temples of the kingdom or religion. At the top of the religious, political, and military hierarchies were key members of the ruling elite class. There was no separation of religion, and kingdom that is characteristic of many large nation states of today. For instance, in the United Kingdom a prince could serve as an army general, a province governor, and a head priest at the same time. This was not viewed as a conflict of interest. (Carneiro: 1981)

Ancient kingdoms were far from being egalitarian. There were a few rich, politically powerful people and many more comparatively poor commoners who had little political influence and almost no possibility of making it. As single-city kingdoms became multi-city empires with vast territories, the political systems generally became more rigid. Not uncommonly, the ruler became a deity-king with absolute authority. The Pharaohs of Egypt are a prime example of this. They were not just mortals but deity-kings. As living deities, their authority was absolute.

Most ancient kingdoms had slavery. The conquest of competitor states or kingdoms usually provided most of them. Slaves were not always at the bottom of the pyramid of power in these societies. In Egypt and Mesopotamia (modern day Iraq, Kuwait, part of Syria, Iran and Turkey), women slaves were often integrated into the households of wealthy and powerful men as servants and concubines. Slave children fathered by their owner sometimes acquired freedom and far higher status, wealth, and power than the commoners.

Some horticultural societies of the past developed more intensive agricultural subsistence patterns when their populations grew into the thousands. As this interrelated economic and population transition occurred, they were forced to create a new level of political integration in order to maintain unity and order. This was the chiefdom and ultimately the kingdom. This marks the beginning of centralized, full-time leadership and non-egalitarian societies. Before examining the nature of chiefdoms and kingdoms, it is important to keep in mind that the political systems in many societies do not clearly and completely fit any of the categories. These horti-cultural societies are essentially in transition from ethnic groups to chiefdoms or from chiefdoms to kingdoms.

Who is a Chief? A chief is a leader of a higher rank – an incumbent of an inherited political role. Chiefs lead because of their ascribed status, not their achieved status.

Types of Chief:

The Paramount Chief is a kingdom chief of a complex chief-dom. Generally, the paramountcy is composed of a central vast kingdom surrounded by a number of towns and smaller subsidiary communities. All of the towns and communities recognized the authority of a single elite group or individual with a vested central power responsible for the entire para-mountcy.

The Town Chief is single simple chiefdom generally com-posed of a converging central community surrounded by or near a number of smaller subsidiary communities and sub-sidiary chiefs. All of the smaller subsidiary communities and subsidiary chiefs recognize the authority of a single elite group or individual with a vested central power, dwelling in the primary community. Each community will have its own leaders, which are usually in a tributary and or subservient relationship to the ruling elite of the primary community.

The Village Chief is single simple chiefdom generally com-posed of a smaller-central community surrounded by or near a number of lesser subsidiary chiefs. The community recog-nize the authority of a single-lesser-elite group or individual

with a vested central power, dwelling in the primary community. Each community will have its own leaders, which are usually in a tributary and or subservient relationship to the ruling
elite of the primary community.

Subsidiary Chief (sub-chief) leads a single complex chiefdom
generally composed of a central community surrounded by
or near a number of smaller subsidiary communities. The
number of structural levels within such chiefdoms is equal, or
more than those within the average kingdom, but they have a
different type of political organization and political leadership.
Such types of political entities do not appear to have been
created by the agriculturists (Kradin 2004). These subsidiary
chiefs are required to function at several levels of equal
capacity. In all the facets of chiefdom, the services of subsidiary chiefs are required to keep the administrative machinery
of their domain going.

The following list represents some of the titles of sub-chiefs
among the Akans of Ghana; *Safeehen* (Head of Key keep-
ers), *Mpɔboahen* (Head of Sandals or Slippers keepers),
Egudzehen; (Head of Ornament or Jewellery keepers), *Atam-
hen* (Head of Cloth keepers), *Fotosamfohen* (Head of
Finance), *Akɔmfohen* or *Kɔmfohen* (Head of Priest or Chief
Priest), *Ntakyrɛhen* (Head of Feathers cap), *Sundzehen*
(Chief of Pillow), *Amankrado* (Chief of Village) *Abrafohen*
(Chief of Executioners), *Asafohen* (Chief of Worrior), *Kyidɔm-
hen* (Head of Real or Home army), *Nyimfahen* (Head of
Right-wing army), *Benkumhen* (Head of Left-wing army),
Gyasehen (Head of Advance team army), *Krontihen* (Chief of
Town), *Apagyahen* (Chief organizer), *Apasemakahen* (Chief
Linguist or Spokesman), *Guantoahen* (Chief Intercessor),
Tufohen (Chief of Musketeer or Gun), *Mbrantsehen* (Chief of
the male Youth) *Mpontuhen* (Chief of Projects and develop-
ment) and other sub-chiefs.

8

Roles of a Chief; the roles of the Chief are fulfilled by the elites who carry out rites and rituals as their preserve. They may also make token, symbolic redistributions of food and other goods at their disposal as and when the need arises. In two-tier or three-tier chiefdoms in which the town and para- mount chief and also the village, town and paramount chief co-relate, higher ranking chiefs have control over a number of lesser ranking individuals, each of whom controls specific territory or social units. Political control rests on the chief's ability to maintain access to a sufficiently large body of tribute (human and material resources), passed up the line by lesser chiefs. These lesser chiefs in turn collect the human services and materials from those below them and communities close to their own centre. At the apex of the status hierarchy sits the paramount chief.

Prohibits of a Chief; the principle of chiefdom upholds total reverence of its subjects and the kingdom. The subjects and sub-chiefs will be cited for contempt if they speak evil and derogatory words about a chief or a higher ranking chief. In addition, the subjects are to pledge their allegiance to the chief and the neglect of this duty may incur the wrath of the chiefdom. *Ntam* or taboos or prohibits are the established prohibitions of any chiefdom. These subjects are therefore not expected to swear against the sorrow and mishaps of the chief and the kingdom, since this may provoke the chief to impose stiffer punishment or custodian sentence on the offender.

Akan chiefdom system is at the apex of a traditional authority system of governance which includes chiefs, queens, sooth- sayers, youth leaders and leaders of various groups together with traditional priests. In addition to their political power, the chief exercises legislative and judicial roles as dictated by the constitution of the Republic of Ghana. In fulfilling their func- tions and ceremonial roles, chiefs and queen-mothers demonstrate the most colourful expression of Ghanaian cultural life especially during festivals and durbars. The prominent chiefs and queen-mothers dress in exquisitely woven cloth *(Kente* or *Edinkra)*, bedecked in gold and beads, and they dance in palanquins at festivals and special occasions.

The umbrella, jewellery, stool and the totem or finial on the staff carried by a chief's entourage denote her rank and role in the hierarchy of power. There are many protocols at the court of the chiefs. Most noticeably, a chief is neither addressed directly nor directly verbally engaged in public, there is always a linguist or a spokesperson through which chiefs address their subjects. The chief as traditional ruler is in the ideal sense, an epitome of decency, uprightness and justice in the community and is accorded great respect. The position is hereditary and in recent times individuals have, formally been elevated to the position of **Mpontuhen** (Chief of Progress and Development) to advance the economic and infrastructural progress and development of a community. Not only have the outstanding citizens of communities been recognised in this way, but many Africans in the diaspora and Europeans have also benefited from the new titles. (Oil-City Magazine, 2003)

It is difficult to ascertain the origin of the chieftancy institution with precision but it is believed that many communities have various systems of governance which far predate colonisation. The status of a chief corresponds almost to the size of the language group she represents and its homogeneity and the wealth and resources at her disposal. For this reason some the rulers are referred to as chiefs while others are known as queens or kings. In Akan kingdom reference is made to the stool of a chief, her en-stoolment or de-stoolment to show its supremacy. Therefore, the stool is the equivalent of the throne and symbolizes the authority of an Akan chief.

Although much power emanates from the office of the chiefs, they are neither absolute in their exercise of authority nor unilateral; every chief, queen or king is advised by a circle of elders (elites) who guide them in public conduct and it is this circle of eminent elders who analyse and decide political issues. They can even de-stool a chief, queen or king. Customary law provides that such people should be king makers.

Why women as Chiefs? For centuries, women have been known to possess qualities that make them good custodians of assets and wealth. In addition, they are also good managers of issues and crises. Although, sometimes very unhesitant in invoking action and decisions on pressing matter, women in most instances make the best judgements and pronouncements. It is in the light of this that among the Akans women form the bedrock of most chieftancy institutions. All over the world women have stood up as beacons of development and governance whether of the traditional African or Western styles. The famous Yaa Asantewaa of Ejuso-Asante, Nana Kofi of Esipon- Sekondi, Nana Fijiaba of Fijai- Sekondi are but a few of the famous females to mention of the Akan chiefdom. This book therefore seeks to hype the female to almost all the natural status of chiefdom even though some of the position especially the executioner is the preserve of males.

In Western Region of Ghana, there are six (6) female chiefs and twenty-three (23) paramount queen- mothers. In the Central Region, Ashanti Region, Eastern Regions which are among the Akan dominated areas of Ghana, females' features as both chiefs and queen-mothers. Some female chiefs are known to have masculine names and titles; a typical example is the chief of Esipon who is named after a masculine name *KOFI, a name for a Friday male born.*

Queen-mothers as title may imply has supervisory role over chiefs. The title queen-mother in Akan could be ascribed to the political mother of the chief. The queen-mothers serve as the political mother of the chief. Both the female chiefs and the male chiefs have queen-mothers attached to their para-mountcy. Although chiefs are associated with the exercise of political authority, queen-mothers play an equally important role in the governance of communities. This has to be under-stood, first of all, within the context of matrimonial society of the Akan where the female line is supreme. The office of the queen-mother *Ɔbaahemaa*, is also a hereditary one and vested with considerable power. Akan queen-mothers are believed to be co-rulers and play a decisive role in choosing chiefs. The proverbial 'OLD LADY' *(Abrewa)* who is referred to in all great decisions by chiefs, reveals the importance of the role of QUEEN-MOTHERS. But among the people of Elmina *(Edinafo)* of the Central Region of Ghana the system for queen-mother does not exist, it is rather the heads of the Asafo Companies *(Akyekuwdu* or *Asafokuw-esoun)* which in this respect act. They have the power to the en-stoolment or de-stoolment of a chief.

In the Akan culture, the highest ranking position is the *Ɔmanhen* (Paramount chief) a term which comes from two Akan words *Ɔman* - traditional area and *Ɔhen* - title for the chief. Both female and male traditional leaders (Chiefs) are addressed as *'Nana'* (a reverential term for age) which is pre-fixed to their stool names. The stool names have weight and are deferent from their real life names. The *Ɔmanhen* has different grades and subsidiary groups of chiefs some of whom have specific functions. These may include chiefs of towns, chiefs of villages and others that may be responsible for welfare, communication, development and warfare. The Akan war formation has, for example, *Gyasehen* who leads and forms the advance guard or vanguard, the *Nyimfahen* who leads the right wing, the *Benkumhen* who leads the left wing and the *Kyidɔmhen* who leads the rear guard.

Contemporary Chieftancy

During the Pre-Ghana period the chieftancy institution became less important and with the introduction of Indirect Rule System by the British Colonialists, chiefs became the conduits of the exercise of the colonial authority. The institution, however, survived this and was resilient to their changing circumstances. Contrary to the view that modern institutions such as the parliament and the court system have come to replace the traditional legislative and judicial roles of the chiefs, the chieftancy institution has become less relevant in contemporary times. *Otumfo Osei Tutu II,* the King (the supreme paramount chief) of the Asanti Kingdom, on the celebration of his fifteenth year celebration of his ascending to the golden stool intimated that the contemporary chieftancy institution has become a necessary institution to promote socio-economic and educational development to her state and community irrespective of the party political system in practice by the state of Ghana. He also mentioned that the chieftancy institution which in the past was very much instrumental in waging ethnic war to expand their frontiers must and has now become the centres for human development, hence his educational fund that has supported and educated over nine thousand brilliant but less endowed citizens of Ghana. Additionally, the king emphasised that numerous legal disputes have been settled in the traditional court system thus reducing the untold pressure on the contemporary courts. The contemporary chieftancy institution can be likened to parliamentary system of governance – interplay of legislative, judiciary and the executive. Recent developments in 1991constitution has vested all natural resources (land, sea, rivers, streams) in the hands of the president on behalf of the people of Ghana rather than the chiefs. Yet the chiefs are the natural custodians of these natural resources. They hold them in trust to their community and state.

In Ghana, the acknowledgement of the chieftancy institution reflects the fact that chiefs must be actively constructive in

contributing to the process of decentralisation, democratiza-
tion and sustainable development. (Country Review Report
and Programme of Action of the Republic of Ghana, Africa
Peer Review Mechanism 2005:142) At the local level, chiefs
conduct their affairs through traditional councils in their juris-
dictional area and are represented at the Regional House of
Chiefs. There are ten (10) Regional Houses of Chiefs, (one for
each region in the country) and a National House of Chiefs
which represents all chiefs and traditional rulers in the country. (Oil-City Magazine 2003)

At the national level the institution and its affairs are regulated
by the Ministry of Chieftancy and Culture. The 1992 Constitution fully recognises and values the institution of chieftancy.
Chapter 22 (section 270)

• The institution of chieftancy, together with its Traditional
Councils is established by customary law and usage is
hereby guaranteed.

• The parliament shall have no powers to enact any law
which-(a) confers on any person or authority the right to
accord or withdraw recognition to or from a chief for any pur-
pose whatsoever; or (b) detracts or derogates in any way
from the honour and dignity of the institution of chieftancy.

Chieftancy is a hereditary institution and queen mothers or
king mothers and chiefs have always been regarded as being
above politics and as mothers and fathers of the communities. Without the protection of the constitution chiefs would
naturally support one party or the other, and this obviously
would have negated the spirit of neutrality chiefs are expected to maintain. Furthermore, party politics is full of personal
insults and ridicules, all of which are believed to be beneath
the dignity of traditional rulers. Similarly, if a situation were to
arise in which a chief participated in politics it would have
been an unfair advantage, therefore the 1992 Constitution
provides in section 270 (1) that; "A Chief shall not take part in

active party politics; and any Chief wishing to do so and seeking election to parliament shall abdicate his stool or skin".

Inheritance

The position of a chief is a life time one and, except in a few instances in which a chief is deemed to have compromised and defiled her or his office. Many chiefs rule until their death, after which, (depending upon the part of the country) their nephews or nieces and sons or daughters could inherit the office or position. Among the Akan people of Western, Central and Ashanti Regions, the inheritance system is matrilineal. This means that the offspring of a chief cannot succeed him or her. In other parts of the country where the patrilineal system operates, a direct offspring could inherit his or her if deemed suitable and within the agreed rotational system of the royal family of the ethnic group or community. Among the Edina traditional people of Central Region of Ghana, the heir to the throne must be a son born at the time the father was on the throne *(Eguaba)*

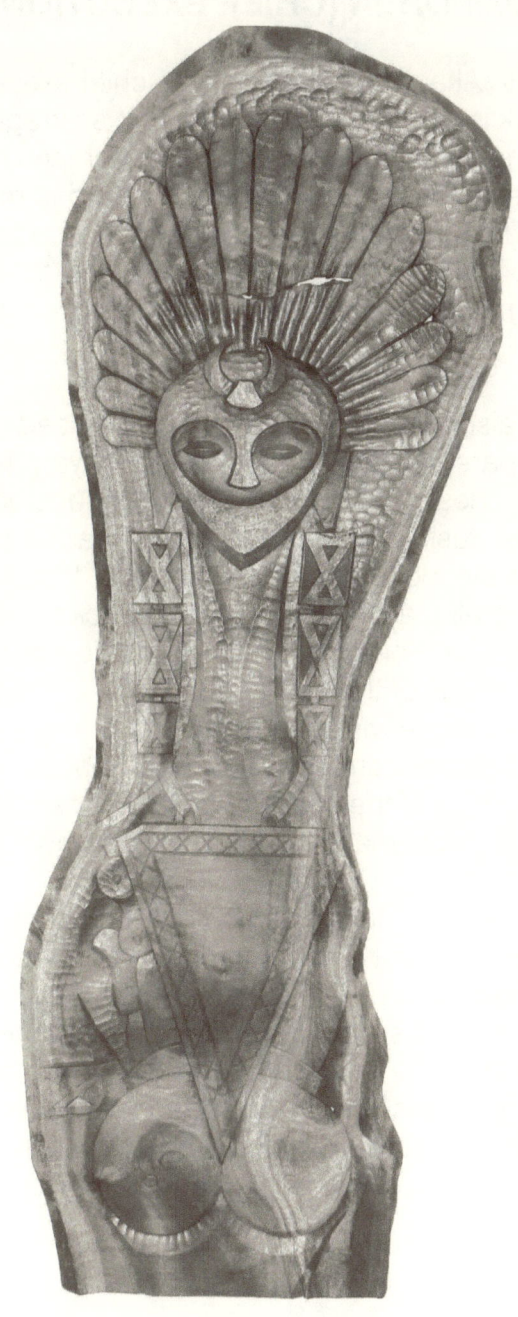

(PLATE: 1)
***EKUMFOHEN* (CHIEF EXECUTIONER)**
WOOD: MAHOGANY, DIMENSION: 140x50x3cm, YEAR: 2002

EKUMFOHEN (CHIEF EXECUTIONER)

Ekumfohen in Akan literally means the chief executioner. This piece of work is a composition made from an irregular Mahogany board that has the upper and lower portions broader and the middle section smaller. The wood board is made of pale red colour. The source of the wood can be traced from a small scale furniture shop where it was selected for the tops of side tables. *Ekumfohen* is a female figure composed with a frontal view.

Ekumfohen also known as abrafohen is dressed in traditional warrior's apparel that consists of a flamboyant head guard, neck guard, chest guard and body suit. In addition there are knives for her task. She wears a pair of ear rings fashioned from *Edinkra* symbol that runs from the ear loop to the shoulder level, and also a simple, but broad neck band. The head guard is in the form of a head helmet and covers the top, side and lower portions of the head and face, leaving only the eye section for effective vision and focus. The top front of the helmet has been decorated with a pair of bull's horns facing each other. Edges of the head guard have been attached with peacock feathers to make it elaborate and imposing.

The eyes, nose and upper portion of the chin have been set in the symbol of heart, but the mouth has been encased as part of the head guard. The long ear rings flag the elongated neck fashioned in a simple neck guard. Below the neck is the chest guard that runs down through in-between the breasts. A pair of executioner's knives is positioned behind the chest guard and within the body suit. The bulging breast set at the lower portion of the composition accents the feminine nature of the executioner.

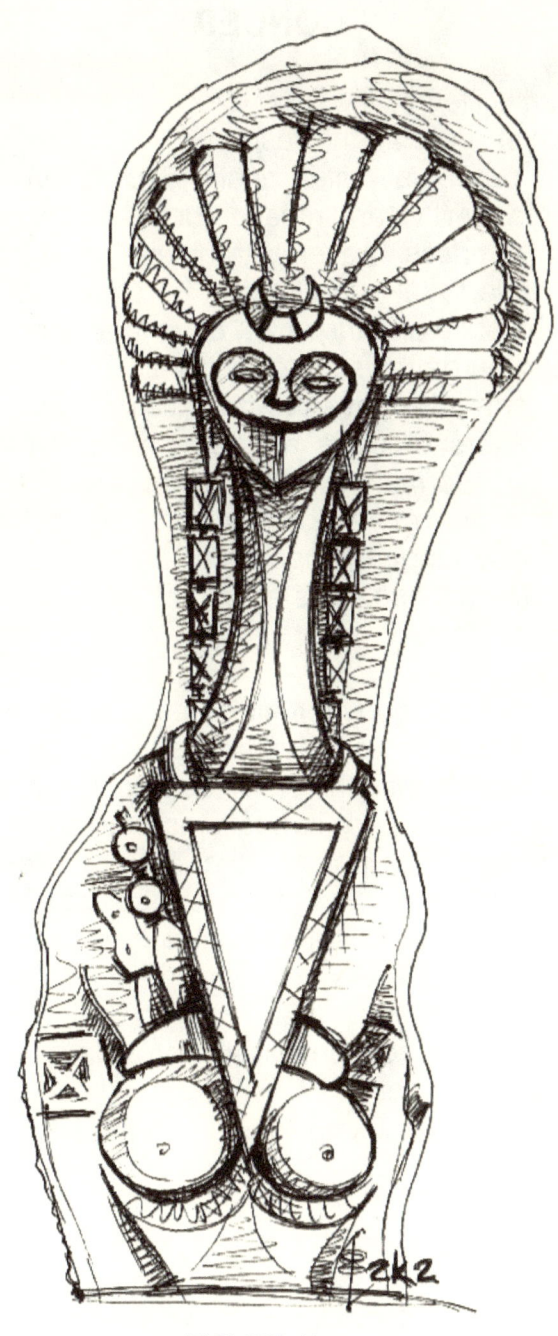

(FIGURE: 1)
***EKUMFOHEN* (CHIEF EXECUTIONER)**

CONCEPT

Ekumfohen is literally the chief executioner of the paramount or town chief and has the responsibility to put persons and convicts to perpetual rest or death. *Ekumfohen* performs the duty for both punitive and ritual purposes. *Ekumfohen* has the qualities of firmness, bravery, sternness, precision and brevity. She is able to take the lives of persons and convicts on behalf of the state and the chief. *Ekumfohen* has the ability to sanitize and purge the state of immorality, of miscreants, misfits and truants who have the potentiality to create fear and panic. A calibre of elites are selected and provided with formal and non-formal education on the execution, precision, bravery, mastery, marshal skills and physical strength. In addition, body language, gestures and facial communications are offered these elites as part of their trade and curricula.

The firm physical body provides assurance, security and strength to attack and subdue all misfits and persons selected for ritual sacrifices. The stern facial look expressed in the art form displays bravery, strength, and the ability of the state to clean herself of all persons that are not to exist and see their evil intentions and wishful destinies come through. The covered mouth conceals the facial and vocal identity of the executioner. It also filters and prevents infection from blood and gases that might emanate from their victim's body. The chest plate has the responsibility to provide protection of the essential organs that exist within the chest cavity. These organs if not well protected could ruin the life and career of the *Ekumfohen.*

In the Akan domain, *edinkra* symbols are symbolic signages that are used to bid good bye to those persons part for the land of the dead or a mission. The inclusion of this signage as part of her adornment indicates her ability to see people off to the land of the dead.

The peacock feathered head guard displays the pride that comes with the practice of the professional-executioner. The executioner ensures the security of the paramount or town chief and the state. The knives popularly known as *daga* or *sipow* ensure the completion of the executioner's task of terminating the lives of their victims. As an assassin, her best job is carried out through the strength of the arms and the body. The firm, mature and athletic figure of *Ekumfohen* is an indication of the enormous energy that originates from her figure. It is therefore crucial that the role of *Ekumfohen* is seen as an important part of the chiefdom in the culture of the Akans.

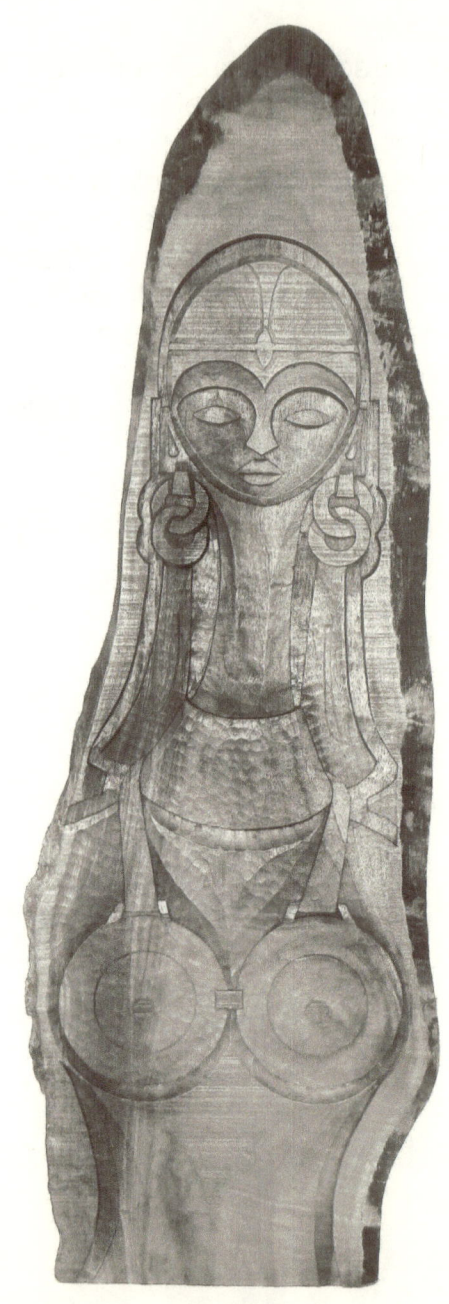

(PLATE: 2)
ASOMAFOHEN (CHIEF MESSENGER)
WOOD: MAHOGANY, DIMENSION: 140x42x3cm, YEAR: 2002

ASOMAFOHEN (CHIEF MESSENGER)

Asomafohen in Akan literally means the chief messenger. This art piece is a composition made from an irregular Mahogany board that has the upper and lower portions smaller and the middle section larger. Asomafohen is a female figure composed in a frontal view. She is dressed in a traditional warrior's apparel that consists of a head guard, neck guard, breast guard and body suit. She wears a pair of ear rings fashioned from *Akomfona*-state sword that runs from the ear loop to the shoulder level. She also adorns her body with a simple, but broad neck band. These ear rings flag the elongated neck and the neck band.

Asomafohen wears a head guard in the form of a head helmet. This covers the top part of the head. The helmet has strings and talisman attached as decoration and as representation of spiritual strength. These strings and talisman run from the top to down and across the bottom section of the helmet. The eyes, nose and mouth are rendered in a simplified realism as natural as possible. The lips of the mouth are fashioned into the archaic smile impression. *Asomafohen* has been adorned with a pair of breast guard that hang from the shoulders. These disc-types of breast guards and the body suit put emphasis on the feminist nature of *Asomafohen*.

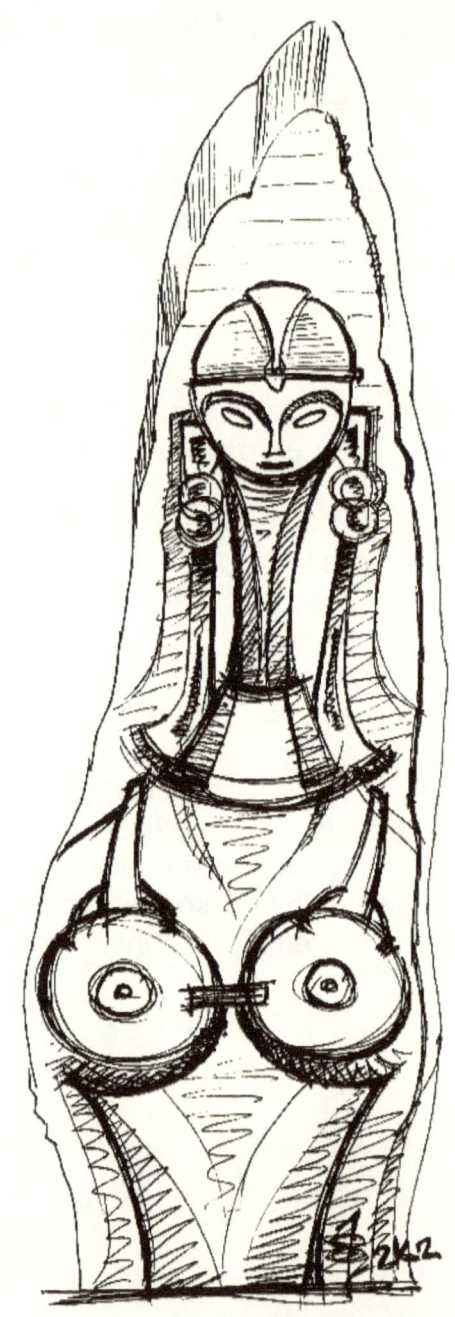

(FIGURE: 2)
ASOMAFOHEN (CHIEF MESSENGER)

CONCEPT

Asomafohen is literally the chief messenger attached to the paramount or town chief. As a sub-chief she has the responsibility of conveying messages to and from the office of the superior chief. In the Akan culture, superior chiefs do not undertake the conveyance of messages to subjects, vassals, and other town and paramount chiefs by themselves. The task of conveyance of messages is done by accredited lower chiefs or elites of the chiefdom who have been educated culturally and formally to perform such august task.

In the culture of Akan chiefdom, messengers are persons with great eloquence, good posture and wisdom of thoughts. They have the qualities of accommodativeness, submissiveness, and receptiveness. They also possess additional qualities of good retentive memory, clarity of thought and have the ability to deliver messages eloquently, expressively and expertly. A calibre of such elites is selected and offered formal and non-formal education on eloquence, mannerism, memory retention and recall skills, as well as body language such as gestures, facial and eye communication as part of their curricula.

Asomafohen has a clear face with an **archaic smile** that suggests the nobility of the chiefdom. The head guard (helmet type) offers the messenger some amount of simplified kinship. The strings and talisman attached to the head provide the figure the needed spiritual fortification and strength required to influence her trade since she may pursue her task through the thick and thin of both the physical and spiritual world. The neck guard protects the neck which is the channel and bridge of the vocal capacity. The neck that holds the head to the rest of the body has been rendered in a firm and cylindrical form. This offers the figure the necessary solidity and strength. Any harm to the head may truncate and discontinue the flow of the message as well as disconnect both ends of the communication. The breast guard create some perfect protection to the chest cavity. These guards protect the chest from any form of physical and spiritual attacks and from the *seen* and the *unseen* worlds. The breathe pattern and vocal strength culminate from the chest of the convener as a result of this, the chest requires some form of protection. These breast guards also protect the very physical breasts that feed and nourish hearers, listeners and benefactors of the chief's messages. These messages are to go a long way to inform, educate and admonish the benefactors.

The state sword worn by *Asomafohen* projects the symbol of authority from which she draws her power – that of the paramount or town chief. Therefore the presence of these replica swords as the ear rings is symbolic of the authority of the chief. Like the adage *let the listening ears listen attentively*. These swords represent the presence of the paramount or town chief at the instance of the messenger. Therefore a disregard and disrespect for the chief messenger is directed towards the superior chief. This will call for punishment or sanctions towards the offender. Display of the elongated neck as well as the slim body figure of the chief messenger fortifies the concepts of elegance and the smartness of her trade-messenger. It may therefore be established that the wise messages that are supposed to be conveyed by the chief messenger resides in her totality as a messenger of the state or kingdom.

In the Akan culture, the human head is seen to be the most important part of the human body; it is noted as the centre for wisdom and knowledge. This therefore calls for the head to be well fortified and protected as the most essential part by the head guard. If the head is not sound then the entire body is unsound. Hence, it is imperative that the *Asomafohen* plays a crucial role within the chiefdom culture of the Akans. The Akan adage says *'se esoma abofraapapa nna asoma wonan',* literally meaning if you detail a person with endowment for an errand then you have completed that errand'. Sending the right calibre of person is more important than any ordinary person.

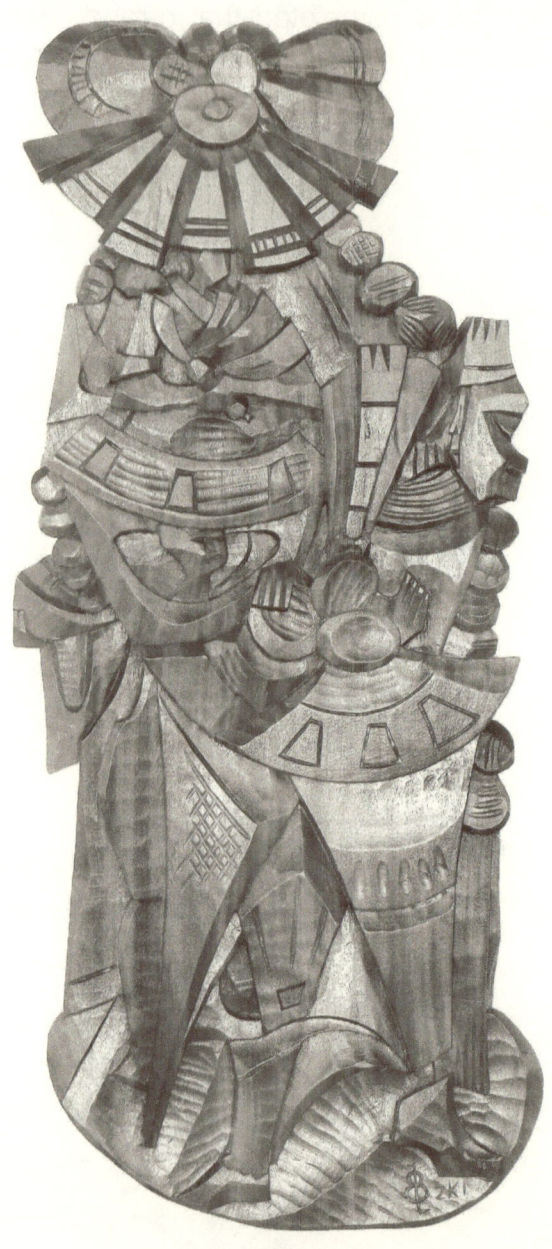

(PLATE: 3)
NKYENHEN (CHIEF DRUMMER)
WOOD: MAHOGANY, DIMENSION: 76x36x3cm, YEAR: 2001

NKYENHEN (CHIEF DRUMMER)

Nkyenhen or *kyerema* in Akan literally means chief drummer. This composition is made from an irregular Mahogany board that has the upper portions smaller, the middle and lower larger. It also has a semi-circular base. The wood board is made up of pale red, yellow and ochre colours. The source of the wood board can be traced to the small-scale saw-mill where it has been selected for future process as domestic furniture material.

Nkyenhen is composed of a lead drummer and other drummers. She is seen performing music and dancing with the sounds from the drums. The musical instrument hangs from her left shoulder. This set of drums is held firmly together by board leather strips that are attached to a single hook unto which they are anchored. The composition embraces the use of concentric, converging and diverging lines as a technique for rendering lines, shapes and forms. The principle of repetition, simplification and linear pattern constitute a major representation of the art work.

Nkyenhen is dressed in a ceremonial war apparel *(Batakeri)* and a head cap. She has her head turned towards the right direction. Behind the *Nkyenhen* are a stool carrier, a dancing chief in a palanquin, horn blowers, a set of umbrellas and several heads belonging to some elites of the chiefdom.

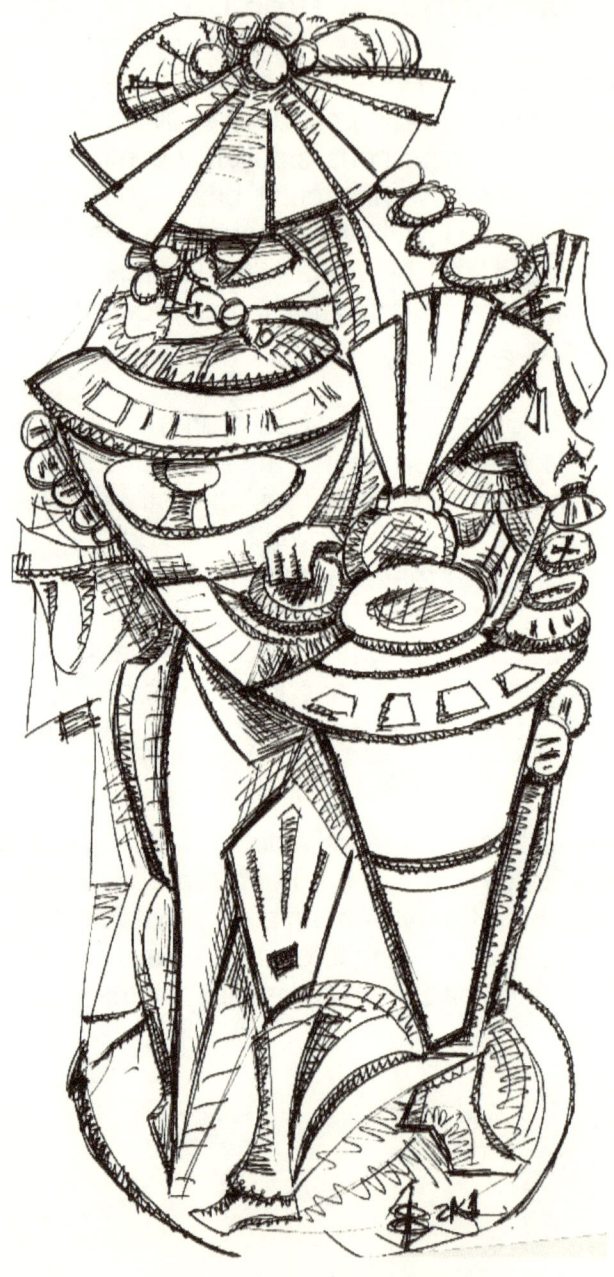

(FIGURE: 3)
NKYENHEN (CHIEF DRUMMER)

CONCEPT

Nkyenhen is literally the chief drummer attached to the para-mount, town and village chief. She bears the responsibility of conveying messages and pieces of information from the chief to her subjects through the use of the drum. This happens especially during festive periods and special occasions. Ordinarily, her core responsibility is to announce to the sub-jects and the inhabitants what is intended to be the wise thoughts and appellations of the chief. In the Akan culture, depending on specific moods and circumstances, the chief drummer leads in the language delivery and presentation of the paramount, town and village chief. For the ability of the drummer to predict and announce the language culture of the chief, the chief drummer is often labelled a divine person.

These drummers are seen as persons with great hands-on-skills and foot-works. They have the flair for con-veying messages, attributes, accolades and appellations in respect of the chiefs. They portray a great sense of humour with gestures and facial expressions during their line of duty. A set of such highly skilled and talented persons is selected from among the elites and at times the commoners and offered formal and non-formal education on sound, music, dance, gestures and humour culture.

The *Nkyenehen* seen in her *Batakeri* dress and head cap depicts her readiness to perform her duty against all odds. Her head, directed towards the right is an indication of her preparedness to provide the right service at the right time on behalf of the chiefdom; an attempt to deliver the message from the chief and possibly translate it to the community. She led the trail of the chief's convoy and attempted to announce the coming of the landowners and repositories of the land-ancestors and deities.

The three drums, three drum strips and three umbrellas in the composition signify the spiritual and the divine anointing bestowed on the chief drummer, hence her accolade *divine-drummer.* As an entertainer and convenor of the paramount, town or village chief her smartness, wisdom and technical prowess are important for the sustainability of the state or kingdom. It is therefore very incumbent that *Nkyenhen* is heavily relied upon in the culture of chiefdom of Akan people, as an announcer, advocate and entertainer. Her services are most sought after.

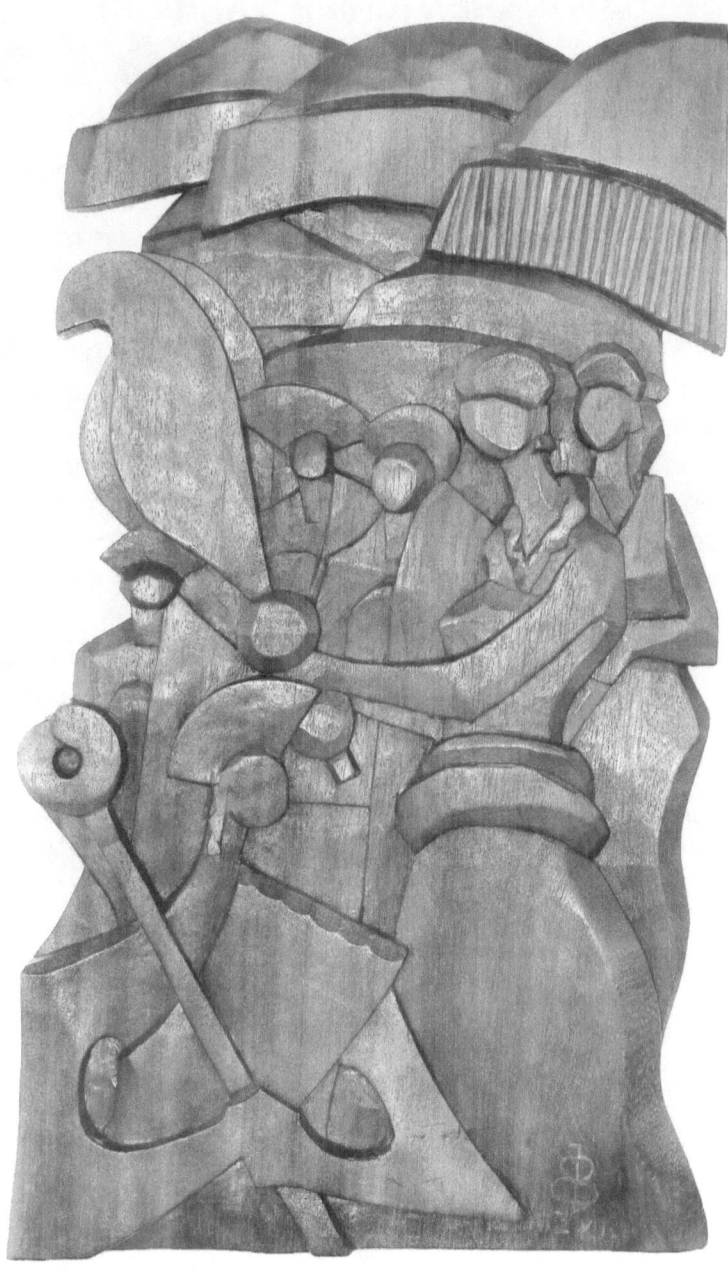

(PLATE: 4)
AFONAHEN (CHIEF WARRIOR)
WOOD: ODUM, DIMENSION: 76x36x3cm YEAR: 2001

AFONAHEN (CHIEF WARRIOR)

Afonahen in Akan which literally means chief warrior is a composition made from an irregular *Odum* wood board that has the lower portion broader than the upper portion. Afonahen may also be called *Sekanhen* or *Osahen*. *Afonahen* is a female figure composed in a three-quarters view holding *Akomfona* (sword or state sword) and in a swearing posture.

She is surrounded by other female sub-chiefs including the chief spokesperson projected in the bust, and positioned at the front bottom of the composition. Behind the figures are a set of umbrella that symbolises the culture of chiefdom of the Akan people. All figures represented in this composition are dressed in the traditional Akan apparel of wrapped cloths above the breasts level and are over the underclothes.

They also have cover cloths that hang from the left shoulders. In addition, they all wear the traditional Akan wig *Tekuwa* over their head as representation of the tradition Akan set up. The *Afonahen*, in this composition is dressed differently. She rather has her cover cloth tied around the waist in readiness for a presumed duty. She has a wreath hung around her neck as an ornament.

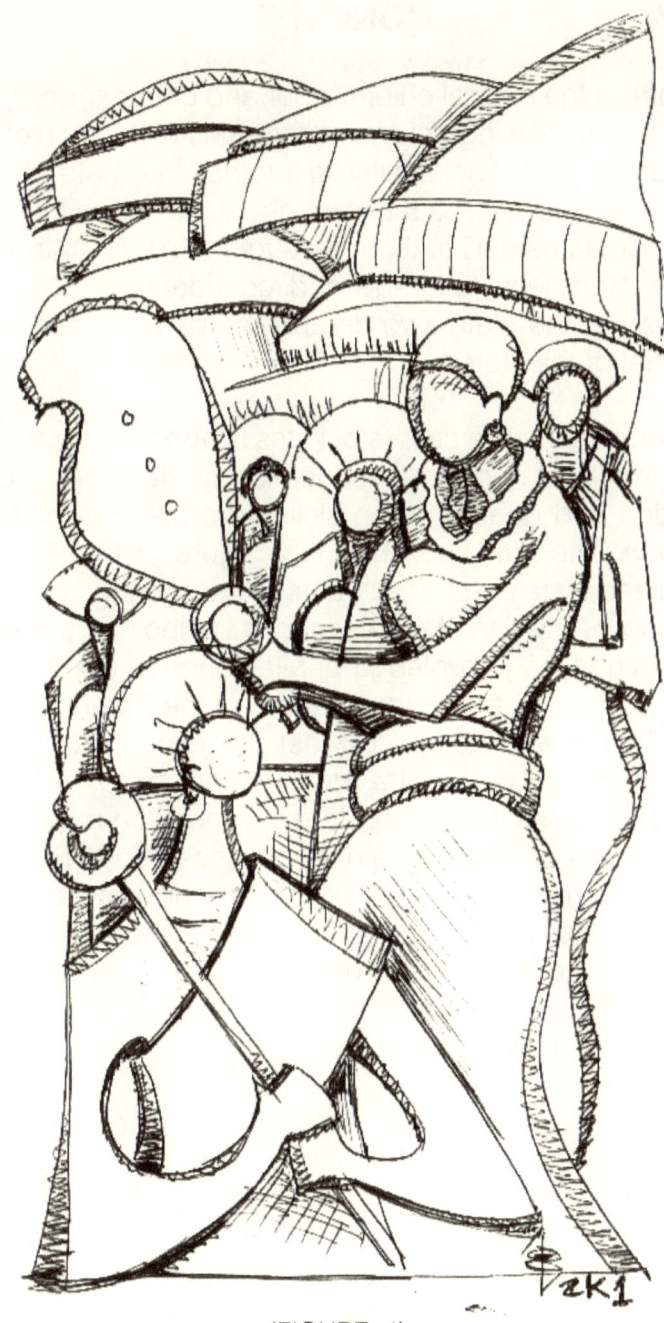

(FIGURE: 4)
AFONAHEN (CHIEF WARRIOR)

CONCEPT

Afonahen is the natural chief warrior and commander general of the military wings of the paramount or town chief. She has the overall responsibility to protect the state and her subject from reprisals, attacks, confrontations and takeovers from other states and authorities. *Afonahen* has attributes of bravery, sternness, courage and confidence. She is the custodian of the state swords and the defence commander-in-chief of the state.

In the Akan culture, a calibre of elites is appointed and given both formal and non-formal education on defence, security, protection and peacemaking skills. She later becomes the *Afonahen.* The firm and able-body figure of the *Afonahen* assures the state and her subjects of the security and physical support. The rise of the *Akomfona* symbolises the *Afonahen's* willingness and pledge of allegiance to the *Ɔmanhen* (paramount chief) the *Ɔman* (state) and the *Ɔmanmba* (subjects). This is an attempt to meet the expectations of the state and the subjects. She has a wreath hung around her neck as an ornament, an act that is synonymous with Akan spiritual leaders. This wreath symbolises *Afonahen's* relationship with the unseen world and the owners of the state as well as the spiritual warriors of the state in the Akan culture. *Afonahen* is depicted in a swearing posture as a symbol of her dominance over her sect and service to the superior leaders of the community.

The various sizes of umbrellas presented in the composition demonstrate the chain of authority under which *Afonahen* serves. The larger the size of the umbrella, the greater the authority the owner possesses. These umbrellas also express *Afonahen's* allegiance to authority and order. The right broad umbrella speaks of a greater authority from which she draws her might and power. She is under the authority and might of the paramount or town chief. She therefore submits to that authority. The lowering of her cover cloth indicates her submission to a higher authority that has respect and honour – Almighty God, deities and ancestors and superior chiefs of the state and town. Lowering of the wrapped cloth as a dress culture is highly practised among the Akan communities in Ghana. This serves as a sign of respect to authority and command. The swearing posture of *Afonahen* is a symbol of her dominance over her sect.

The presence of the chief linguist and all persons cited in the composition act as witness to the ceremony as the *Afonahen* pledges her support and commitment to the custodians and owners of the state. The swearing procedure is a testimony that cannot be abandoned. It is therefore important that *Afonahen* does all things to ensure security of the state and her subjects.

The wearing of *Tekuwa* (a traditional wig) over the heads of the figures is a representation of the female traditional set up among the Akans. In Akan, the physical strength of females is demonstrated by tying a cover cloth across their waist. This is to secure the proper holding of their wrapper cloth in order to prevent their loosening up and exposing their nudity. The *Afonahen* therefore has her cover cloth tied around the waist in readiness for a presumed battle or duty. The wreath worn around *Afonahen's* neck as an ornament, establishes her association with the spiritual world and their leaders. Wreath symbolises a relationship with the unseen world. As a warrior of the Akan people, she equally requires the spiritual strength and connection to perform her assignment. It is therefore worth having the *Afonahen* as part of the culture of chiefdom of the Akan people.

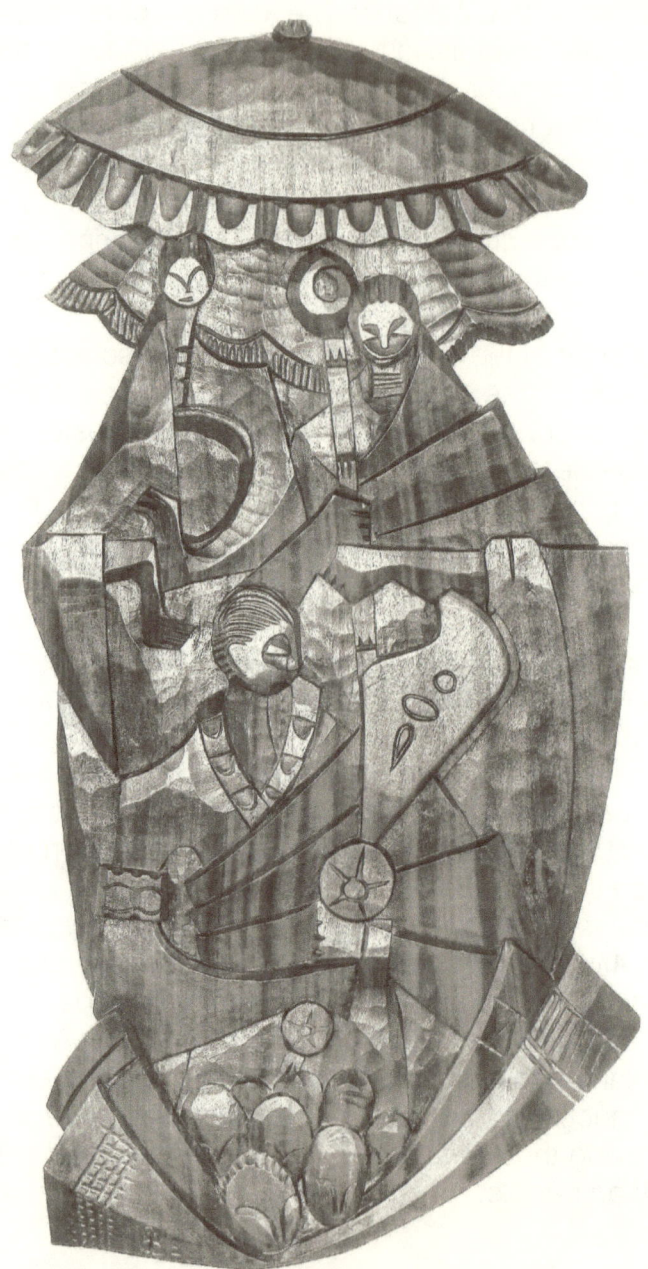

(PLATE: 5)
MPONTUHEN (DEVELOPMENT CHIEF)
WOOD: SAPELE, DIMENSION: 76x36x3cm, YEAR: 2001

MPONTUHEN (DEVELOPMENT CHIEF)

Mpontuhen in Akan literally means Developmental or Progress Chief. This is a composition made from an irregular
Sapele wood board that has a semi- circular top and bottom
shapes and straight middle section. The source of the Sapele
wood board can be traced to the small-scale saw where it
has been selected for future process as domestic furniture
material. *Mpontuhen* is a composition of a youthful female
surrounded by two other female elites positioned behind her.
It has a group of horn blowers set in the front roll. *Mpontuhen*
is posed in a three quarter posture and looks forward; the
members of the community. The composition makes do with
radiating and converging technique of composing lines,
shapes and forms. The top portion of the composition depicts
a set of two umbrellas.

A highly generous and project–oriented person is selected
from among the youth to be offered the status of an elite.
Mpontuhen does not need to be a member of the elite community, rather it is her generosity and social centred motiva-
tion that may earn her the elite status. She is taken through
formal and non-formal education on mannerism, speech and
dance gestures. In the composition, the figure on the rear
right, the chief linguist is dressed in traditional apparel that
starts from the chest. She holds a state mace that has the
Sankɔfa crafted finial sitting on top of a decorated pole. The
figure on the rear left of the queen-mother is also dressed in
the traditional female chief's apparel. She is in a hand clap-
ping posture. Both rear figures are seen expressing the joy of
acclamation towards the swearing activity. At the bottom part
of the composition are a group of horn blowers popularly
called "*Mbεn esoun*". *Mbεn* in Akan means horns (wind
instrument) and *Esoun* means a team of seven players. The
horns "*mbεn*" are distributed on both sides of the composition and are spread across the bottom part.

Mpontuhen is dressed in a typical Akan apparel for chief-dom with elaborate jewellery around the neck, arms and wrist. She wears a braided hair style that stretches back-wards. She is in a solemn mood and holds in her both hands '*Akomfona* – a state sword used for oath taking. It is also the symbol of her office.

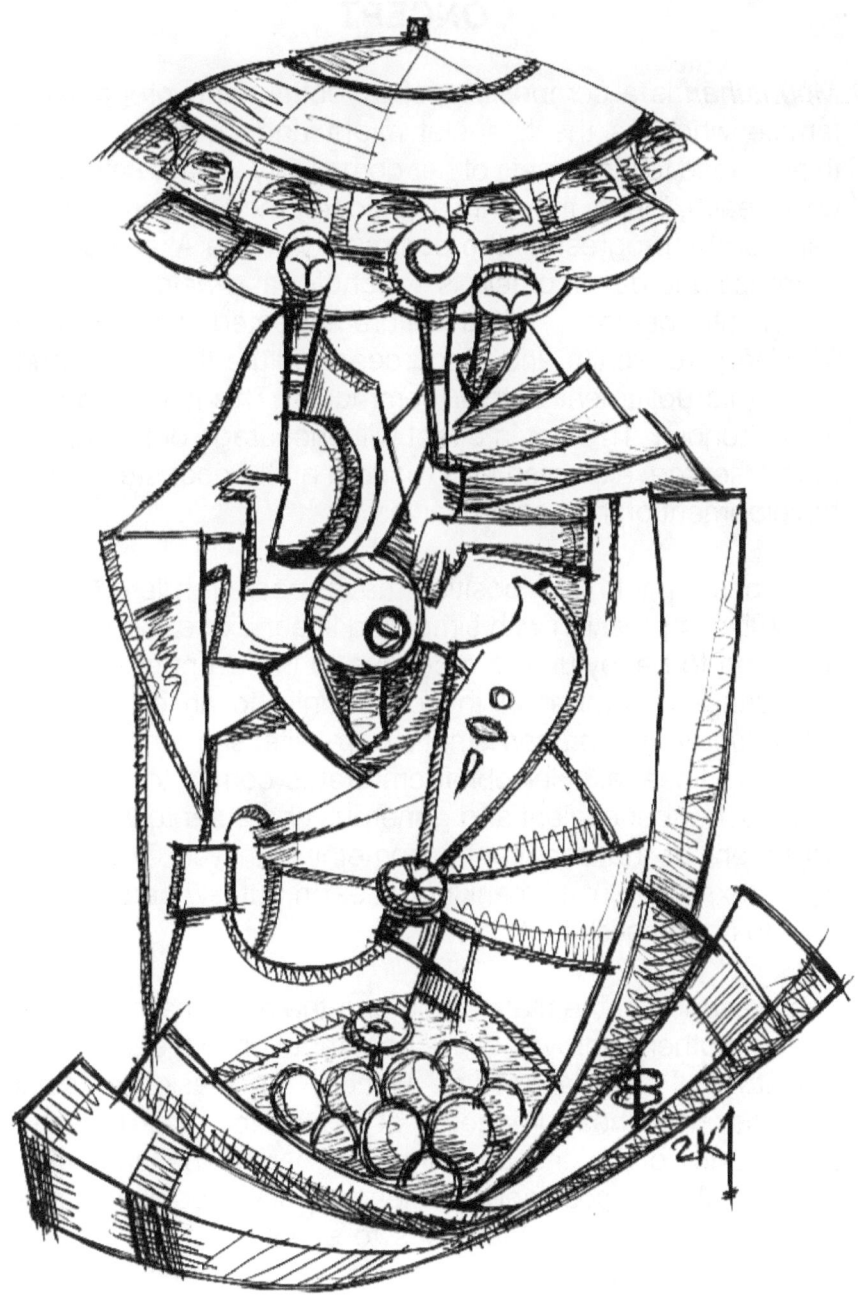

(FIGURE: 5)
MPONTUHEN (DEVELOPMENT CHIEF)

CONCEPT

Mpontuhen is a composition of a youthful and progressive female who has the financial might and charisma to get things done to the benefit of her community. She is saturated with wealth, ideas, thoughts and good omen that are significant for the progress of the community. In the Akan culture, progress and development is sought for and welcome by all meaningful persons. It is therefore expected of all persons who acquire wealth and resources to allure the social and economic upliftment of their community. This is considered as an honour. This act in effect will encourage others to put their resource, expertise and wisdom at the door step of the development of their communities.

All faces in this composition have been rendered in a mask-like impression with simplified linear expression. They are seen to be joyful and receptive to the event of the day, honouring a member of the community to an elite status '*Mpontuhen*'. *Mpontuhen* is not a born elite; she is not born to the royal lineage. Her chiefdom status comes to her as a result of her benevolent and generous character towards the upliftment of the community, something that is God given and is expected of all mankind on earth but few persons are able to accomplish that.

The presence of the state mace and the acclamation by the queen-mother approves of their contribution to the state and the stool of their ancestors. Hence, the mask-like facial expression of these images that signify the approval and acceptance of the unseen spirits – owners of the land. Likewise, the *Mbɛn esoun* and their leader positioned at the base of the composition further goes to show the stool and the announcement of the elevation of a 'commoner' into the status of an elite. This gives an indication that the state and the stool are ever ready to honour and appreciate all persons who are ready to devote themselves and their genuine

41

resources for the development and upliftment of the state, community and individuals.

The umbrella positioned over *Mpontuhen* symbolizes her new role and authority. This is enjoined with that of the Ɔ*man-hen's,* making the appearance of the two umbrellas at the top of the composition (Ɔ*manhen* and *Mpontuhen*), a force worthy for the progress of a state or community

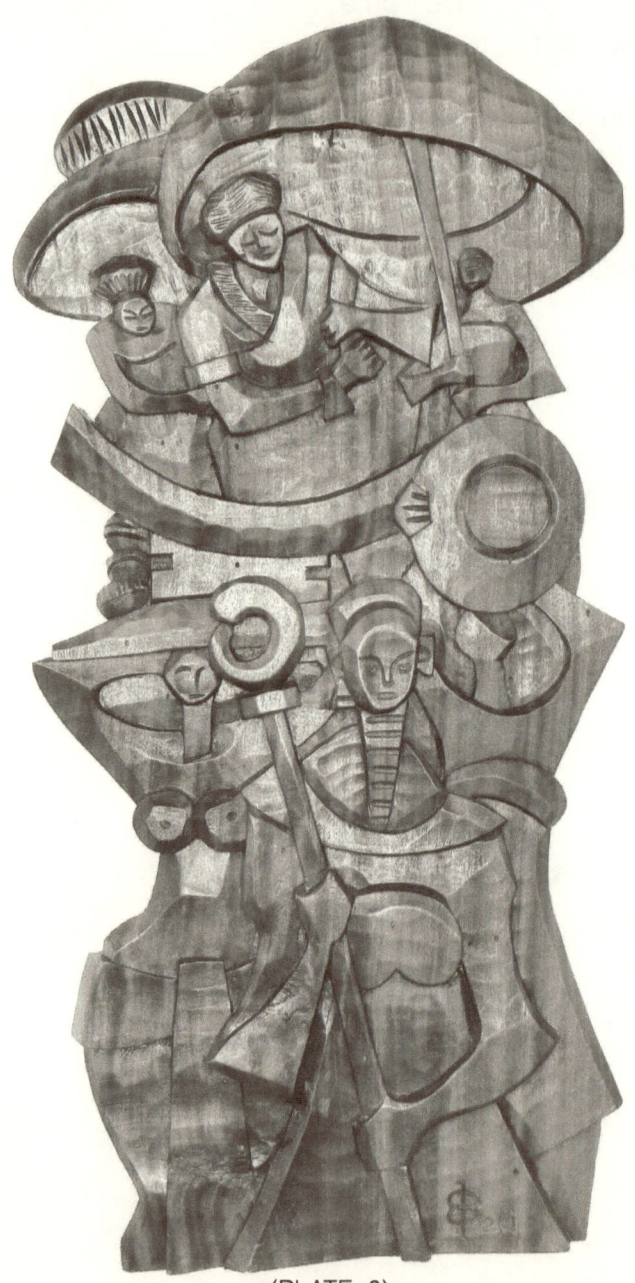

(PLATE: 6)
AKYEAMEHEN (CHIEF LINGUIST)
WOOD: SAPELE, DIMENSION: 76x36x3cm, YEAR: 2001

AKYEAMEHEN (CHIEF LINGUIST)

Akyeamehen in Akan literally means the chief linguist or chief spokesperson of the paramount or town chief. This is a composition made from an irregular Sapele wood board that has jagged edges at both sides of the wood board, a semi-circular top portion and a horizontal base. The source of the Sapele wood board can be traced to the small-scale sawn where it has been selected for future process as domestic furniture material. *Akyeamehen* is composed of a female figure that holds in both hands a mace positioned across her body. The mace has a *Sankɔfa* finial that sits on top of a simple, non-decorated wooden stave. She is leading an envoy made of a paramount chief who sits and dances in a palanquin accompanied by other elites of the paramountcy.

Akyeamehen is dressed in a traditional Akan '*Kaba*' top and wrapper cloth. She wears a broad but simple choker jewellery around her neck. She is followed closely on the left by the carrier of the paramount chiefs' stool. She is dressed from the traditional *Amoanse* enhanced underwear made of *duukuu* (head scarf cloth) and *serekye Amoanse* (silk cloth) worn as the lowering cloth wrapped around beads fixed at the waist of a female. She has nude body which exposes her breasts that has invert nipples. *Akyeamehen* is again followed closely to the right by the carrier of the chief's food and drinks. She is dressed in the traditional Akan casual attire of a wrapper cloth above the breast that flows from the chest section to the knees. Behind these figures is the dancing chief. The dancing chief is also closely followed by the umbrella bearers to the right and the supporter of the hand of the dancing chief. Both rear figures are also dressed in the traditional casual attire of wrapped cloth tied around the chest and rounded down to the knees. Behind these figures is the composition of three umbrellas of varied sizes, openings and shapes. All figures are rendered in linear, detailed

44

representation.

In the Akan culture, chiefs do not speak openly and directly to people and their subjects without a mediator. Also, a chief does not speak aloud and vigorously in public. There is always a spokesperson who echoes and re-sounds the thoughts and mind of the chief. Spokespersons are accredited elected person who may not necessarily be members of the elites but have an outstanding, wisdom, oratory skills, eloquence, honour and clear thought of presentation and recall.

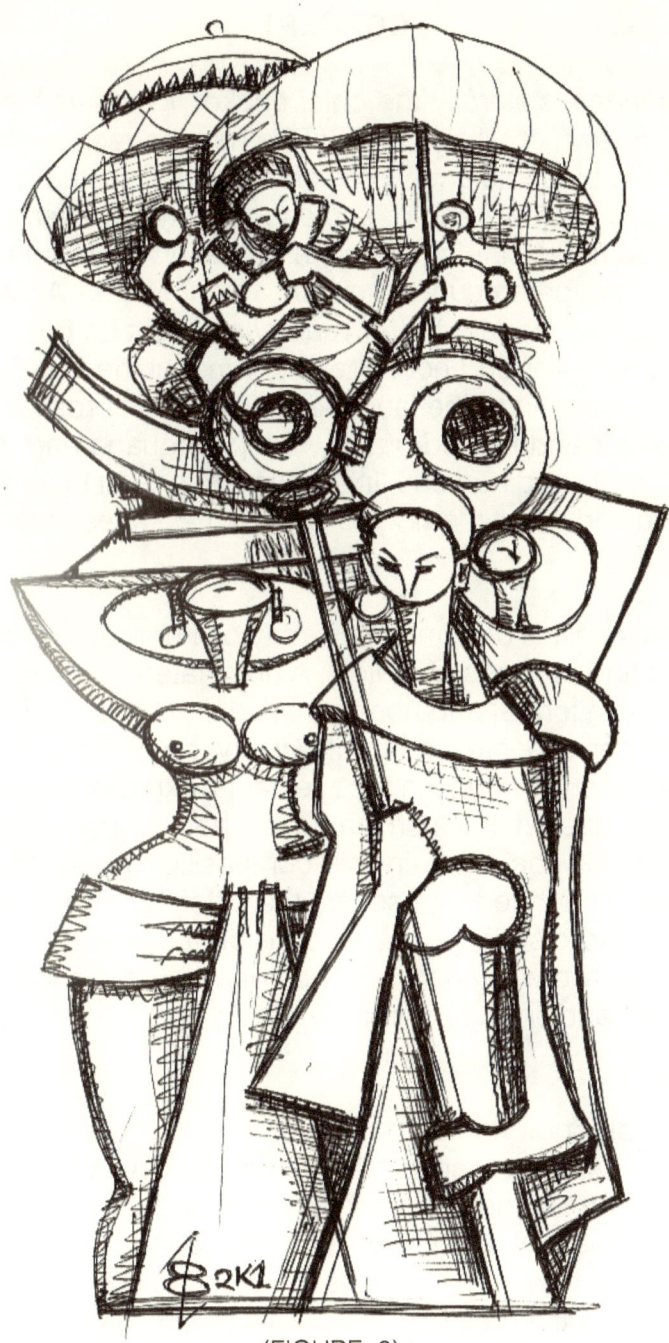

(FIGURE: 6)
AKYEAMEHEN **(CHIEF LINGUIST)**

CONCEPT

Akyeamehen is literally the chief spokesperson of the paramount or town or village chief. She has the responsibility to deliver the thoughts and words of the chief – custodian of the land to the subjects and or audiences. *Akyeamehen* has the duty to communicate an oratory and preserve the dignity and sanity of the paramount or town or village chief. An error of speech committed by the *Akyeamehen* might be deemed as an error from her and not necessarily that of the Chief, Landlord or Custodian of the land. *Akyeamehen* possesses qualities of clear and refined oratory, deep language and idioms, speech skills and humour. In addition, she must have a good retentive and recall memory to convey messages to and from the chief.

A calibre of elites or commoners may be nominated based on wisdom and prowess of oratory. A nominated person shall be offered both formal and non-formal education to equip her to perform her expected duty with clarity, precision and decorum. Additionally, body language, facial expression and gestures are offered the nominated as part of her vocational curricula. Akyeamehen, in this composition presents a firm and solid structure that assures the chief and other elites of her ability to discharge the responsibilities that is bestowed on her; the two-way channel of communication – chief to subjects and audience and from subjects and audience to the chief.

The simple but non-elaborate and broad neck jewellery placed around the neck of Akyeamehen serves as the yoke that exists to abide by the command and control from the superior chief. Like the yoke attached to the neck of a farm oxen or donkey that restrains and controls their activities according to the master's wish. This ornamental yoke seeks to direct and restrain the Akyeamehen to the wishes and dictates of the superior chief or that of the town and village chief. The mace literally known as the linguist staff is the symbol of the office of Akyeamehen. The mace is part of the embodiment of the chief; it connotes the presence and supremacy of the paramount, town or village chief. There-fore, the procession of the mace by the *Akyeamehen* con-firms the authority and power vested in her by the custodians of the land. She acts on behalf of them. It is therefore inferred that any negative action or treatment meted on the *Akyeame-hen* is an action to the custodians as well. She is therefore respected, honoured and listened to by subjects and audi-ences as the representative of the custodian of the land.

The presence of the nude figure as the carrier of the chief's (paramount or town chief) stool identifies the paramountcy with purity, sanity and sanctity. In the Akan culture, the spiri-tuality of the chief is manifested in a virgin. Since virgins have no carnal knowledge; it is therefore essential for the sanctity of the stool to be protected by people who are naturally sanc-tified. In effect, spiritual potency is injected into the person carrying the stool. This spiritual potency of the paramountcy backs the activities of *Akyeamehen* since she is duly support-ed by the paramountcy.

The carrier of the pot which contains food and drinks takes care of the safety of the food, hygiene and whatever goes into the physical body of the chief. She provides food energy for the physical wellbeing of the paramountcy. It is therefore imperative to receive support from such an important member of the elite (pot carrier) by *Akyeamehen* to keep her duties and activities going.

The two figures beside the paramount chief umbrella bearer and carrier of arm (hand) exist to provide support and protec-tion to the physical being of the chief. Generally, chiefs are protected from harsh sun rays. Due to the weight of the jewellery in their dresses, it becomes necessary to offer some support to the arms (hands). Such elites extend their support to *Akyeamehen*. Whatever is due to the paramountcy trickles down to sub-chiefs and the elites. Sources of authority of chiefdom are mostly seen in the type and size of the umbrella available to the chiefdom. It is a common place knowledge that "the bigger the umbrella the higher the rank and status of a chief". This applies to the decoration at the edges and top of the umbrella. The adage *"ahemfo kyem ebi dze ebi ekyir"* meaning – "the bigger your authority the bigger the umbrella". Some umbrellas are in two and three tiers. Therefore the authority of *Akyeamehen* is seen in the appearance and presence of the umbrella and the mace.

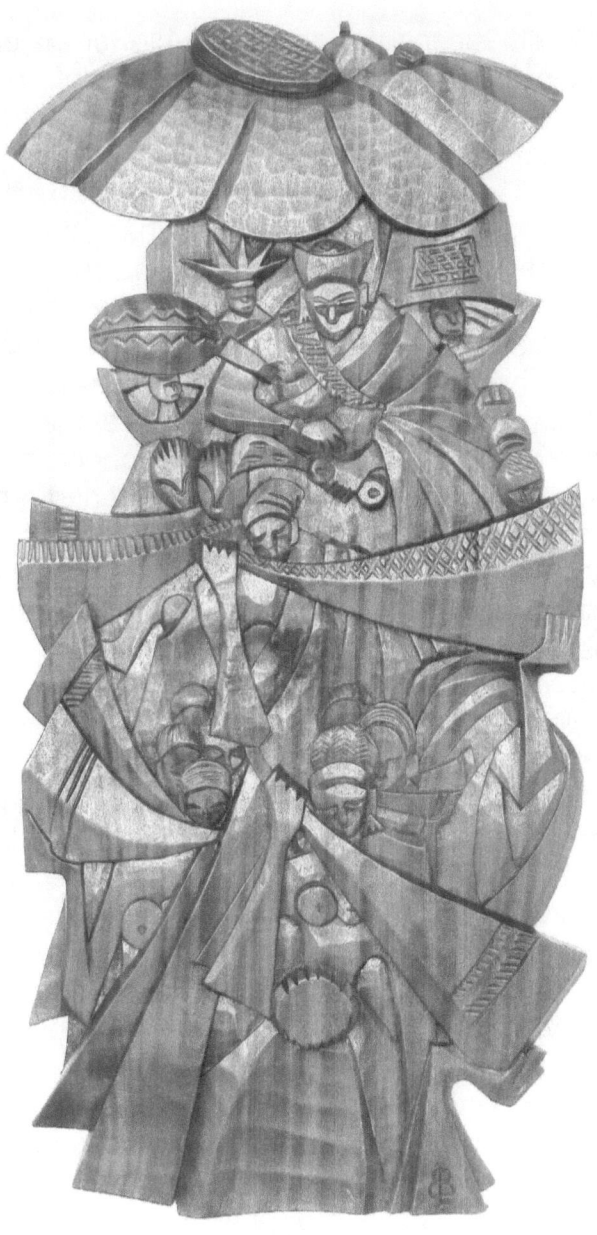

(PLATE: 7)
MBƐNHEN (CHIEF HORN BLOWER)
WOOD: SAPELE, DIMENSION:76x 36x 3cm, YEAR: 2001

MBƐNHEN (CHIEF HORN BLOWER)

Mbɛnhen literally means the chief horn-blower or leader of horn-blowers of a paramount, town or village chief. This relief sculpture is fashioned from an irregular Sapele wood board that has a narrow top and bottom portion and a broader middle portion. The source of the Sapele wood board can be traced to the small-scale saw-mill where it has been selected for future process as domestic furniture material. *Mbɛnhen* may be known as *Atentebenhen* or *Abentsefohen* This composition consists of several horn blowers from the lower portion about two-thirds the height of the board. *Mbɛnhen* – the chief horn-blower is positioned in the centre of the composition. She is dressed in the usual Akan wrapper cloth and a cover cloth which drips from the left shoulder and arm. She also wears an Akan *'Densinkran'* royal hair style associated with elderly person and also used for festive occasions. The hair style has a raised top hair and a low hair-cut around the preferences of the hair section of the head.

Mbɛnhen holds in her hands the largest and elaborate horn. The supporting blowers hold varied sizes of horns. All the horns in the composition are positioned almost in horizontal position and are spread towards the left and right direction. The supporting horn blowers in the composition are dressed in the traditional form, showing the bare chest over wrapper cloths fixed from their waists. This form of dress is associated with giving reverence to Almighty God, the deities, ancestors and other supernatural beings. It is also synonymous with the culture of chiefdom of the Akans. The upper portion of the composition consists of the paramount chief seated in a palanquin and dancing with the *Akomfona* – state sword in the right hand. The paramount chief is surrounded from the left by the carrier of the chiefs' apparel (jewellery and cloths) and to the right by the carrier of the state stool upon which the chief sits.

51

Behind the dancing chief is the *Akɔmfohen-* the spiritual leader, the royal priest and the mediator of the Unseen and the Seen. She wears on her head a natural braid, something that is likened to that of Samson in the Bible. Above these figures are a set of three umbrellas with varied sizes, shapes and forms. All the three figures surrounding the chief are dressed in the partial top-nude. The paramount chief is dressed in a gorgeous chiefly apparel of head crown, neck band, arm bands and ear-rings- an outfit that makes the chief superior to her subordinate chiefs and subjects.

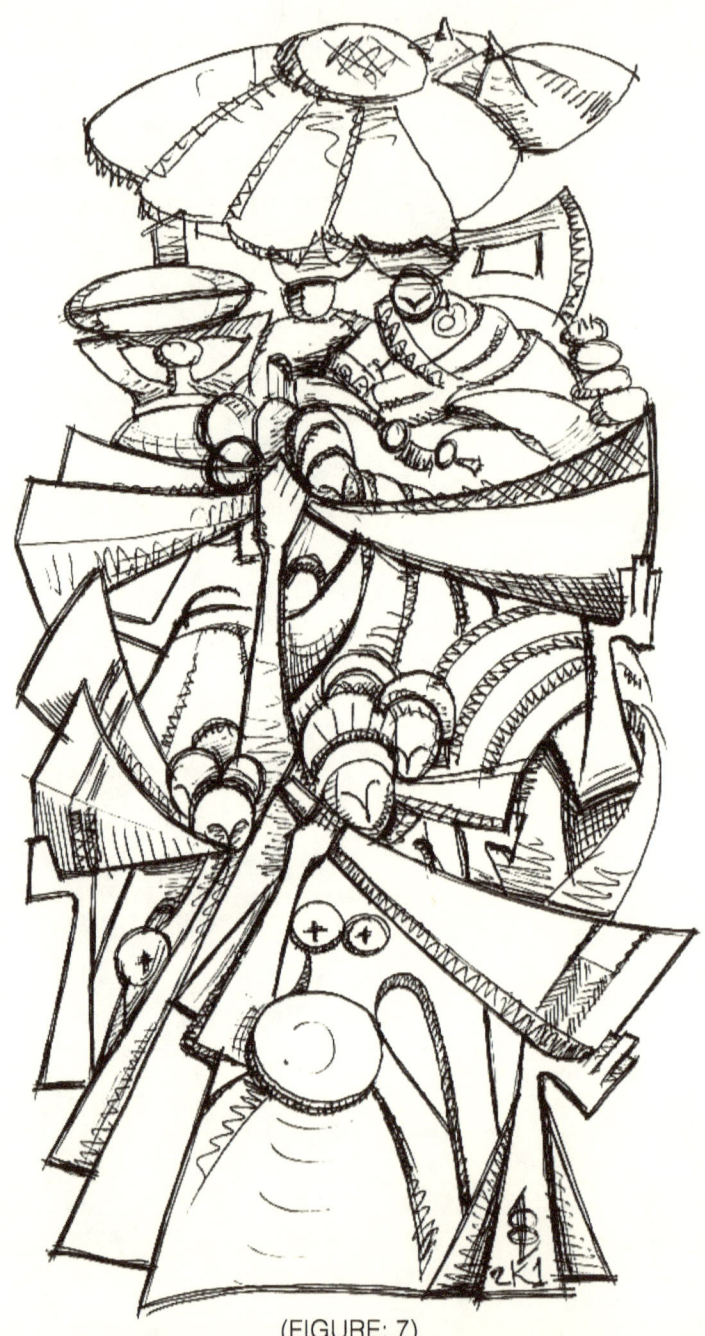

(FIGURE: 7)

MBƐNHEN (CHIEF HORN BLOWER)

CONCEPT

Mbɛnhen is the vector and courier of the pronouncement of action of the paramount chief (declaring war) to the subordinate chiefs and subjects. In the Akan language culture, the horn resonates the appearance or presence of the Lord(s) of the land, and initiates a sudden, immediate and intended action. Therefore, chiefs do not appear in state without the blown sound of horns.

Horn or tusk patronized by Akans is usually fashioned from animals that possess enormous strength and might. Horns or tusks of Elephants, Bull, Rhino, etc are preferred for the production of such wind instrument of music. The sound produced by a horn depended on the type and nature of the animal from which the instrument is fabricated. These are animals seen as possessing some enormous power and strength; their horns are therefore deemed as power-symbols of the chiefdom. These horns are used in reflection of the strength and might of the chiefdom or state. Their power and strength therefore resounds the quest for royal trails to be led by the army of horn blowers.

During royal trails, chiefs may as a matter of fact change over or redress in a more expensive and elaborate apparel in order to undo a challenge posed by subordinate chiefs and wealthy subjects. In the Akan culture a paramount chief must not be out-dressed by a lesser chief or subjects since paramount or senior chiefs are presumed to be the custodians of wealth and property of the state or town. Therefore, the presence of the courier of the chief's apparel expresses the readiness to recover dignity and look of the chief.

It is generally a belief that, chiefs do not sit in palanquins forever. The tendency is for them to be well and properly seated in state. The presence of the stool and her carrier in the composition expresses the preparedness to get the chief duly seated and relaxed while in state. State stools are the repository of the spirits of ancestors and elders. Therefore, the appearance of the stool at the state functions connotes the presence of the ancestor and elders at a gathering. The Akans believe that a chief without a stool never exists. Spirituality and spiritism within the ranks of the chiefdom is potent and extreme. All chiefs are properly protected and fortified by their spiritual team usually led by the *Ɔman Kɔmfo*–state priest or the chief priest. The presence of *Ɔman Kɔmfo* as a background to the paramount chief is an expected practice among Akans.

Umbrellas portrayed at the top portion of the composition expresses the symbol of the supremacy, rank and wealth of chiefs. Umbrella finials, colours, fabrics, staves, shapes and forms speak volumes about the status and level of affluence of one chief over another. The presence of the paramount chief, at the upper part of the composition and her umbrella signifies the support of the paramount chief as well as her supervisory role over the activities of *Mbɛnhen* as a subordinate chief to the elites. In this composition, the paramount chief is gorgeously dressed in the Akan chief's apparel that includes, head crown, neck band, arm band and ear-rings. She holds the *Akomfona* – state sword which serves as her symbol of office, authority and power. The *Mbɛnhen* is equally dressed to the standard of a chief, very large wrapper cloth that drips downwards. Her large decorated Abɛn (horn) identifies her as the chief horn blower and leader of the *Abɛnbɔfo*- horn blower. She supersedes the activities of the *Abɛnbɔfo* and relates to the paramountcy and the community members through the wind instrument *Abɛn*-horn. As an elite of the community, her major responsibility is to provide better image and dignity for the chiefdom.

The *Abɛnbɔfo* have their upper torso exposed. This exposure or partial nudity is quite symbolic. They offer themselves to the leadership, elders and ancestors of the community with some amount of humility, respect and honour. In the Akan culture, virginity and nudity are means through which appeals and reverence is sort for. The Akan leader will have to lower her wrapper cloth from around the shoulder as a sign of humility towards the unseen and superior members of the community. This lowering of cloth provides some degree of nudity to the upper body done by the *Abɛnbɔfo*. It is recognized that the carriers of ornament, and stool as well as the spiritual leader are all dressed in this partial nudity. The vitality provided by the youth through the exposure of the breasts and upper torso goes to expatiate on the virginity, sanity and purity of the paramountcy as well as the community and the unseen members.

It is imperative that the composition relates to the chiefdom in connection the spiritual potency derived from the spirits of the animals that provided the horns, the spirits of the ancestors, the deities and the Almighty God and that of the living. Hence, the concept of nudity and horn blowing uplifts the spiritual and physical wellbeing of the community.

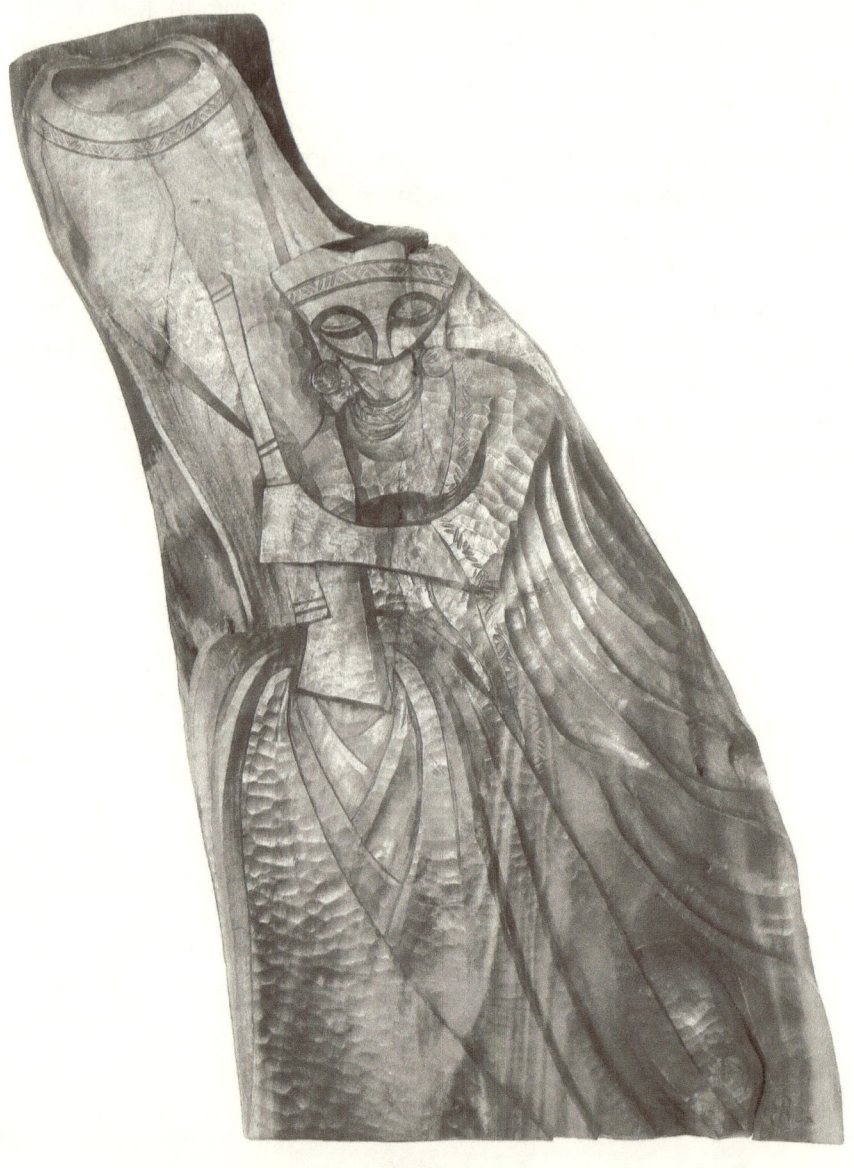

(PLATE: 8)
DEWURHEN (CHIEF GONG-GONG BEATER)
WOOD: BLACK MAHOGANY, DIMENSION: 145x71x5cm, YEAR: 2013

DEWURHEN (CHIEF GONG-GONG BEATER)

Dewurhen in the Akan culture literally represents the Chief gong-gong beater. *Dewur* is that traditional metal musical instrument popularly called gong-gong. It usually has one or more openings. This composition is produced from a black mahogany irregular board that has a narrow top portion, wider middle portion and a chamfered lower portion. The board has the upper portion display of a jugged edge with tree bark and sap. The lower portion has end split while the middle portion contains traces of knot spots. The source of the mahogany wood board can be traced to the small-scale wood market where it has been selected as wood fuel for food production.

Dewurhen showcase a female adult beating a gong-gong. She is dressed in a contemporary traditional apparel of a cover cloth (cloak) over blouse and wrapper cloth. She wears a head crown, elaborate ear-rings and necklace decorated with linear pattern from traditional motif. Her cover cloth has on the periphery the same linear pattern as that of the ear-rings. The cover cloth drapes from the shoulder of the figure. The left side of the cover cloth exhibits a windy-flow drapery while that of the right projects an inter-lace of a care-fully woven drapery from the elbow joint of the right arm. Both sides of the cover cloth merge into the base of the composition creating a unified band of concentrated linear pattern.

Dewurhen, holds in his hand a large *Dewur* (gong-gong) that has a single opening that faces upwards. Her left hand holds that stick used to strike the dewur upon which the sweet sound is created. *Dewurhen* is positioned in a frontal view with the bulging eyes slightly opened. The lower portion of the composition is fully carved. This complements the upper portion of the composition that projects the tree bark and jagged edges of the wood board. *Dewurhen* wears a solemn face that is reflective of deep thought and speech. She has the responsibility to echo and announce the thoughts, words and powers of the paramount chief over the subjects and community.

As an announcer of the thoughts and words of the leaders of communities and the unseen world, the posture of the *Dewurhen* in this composition reflects tradition of the message versus the messengers. As a chief announcer to the seen and the unseen, she is expected to possess the following qualities: eloquence, humour, thrills, poetry, humility, nobility and elegance.

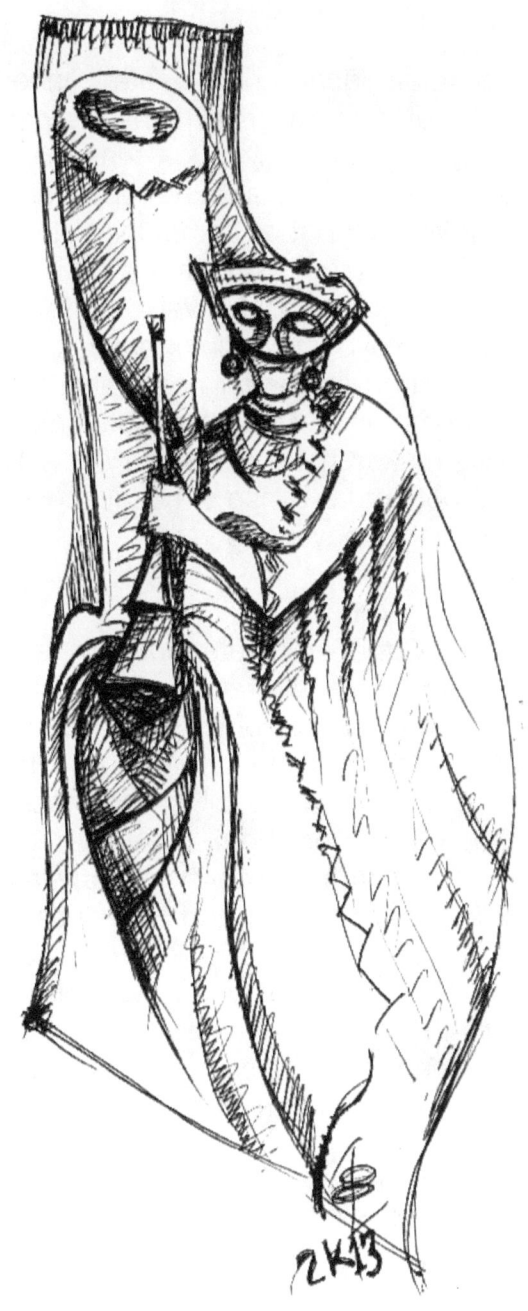

(FIGURE: 8)
***DEWURHEN* (CHIEF GONG-GONG BEATER)**

CONCEPT

Dewurhen, the chief gong-gong beater, announcer and a convener of thoughts and words, holds the concerns of the physical and spirit worlds. Through Almighty God, deities, ancestors, benevolent spirits and the repositories of the customs and traditions of the community, the vocation of gong-gong beating and announcement of vital information is achieved at the community level. Traditionally, as the announcer and conveyor of vital information of the community leaders, she is bound to appear noble and calm before her audience and community. *Dewurhen* puts on a solemn facial expression and makes her eyes bulge out a bit in order to make her face connote a sense of seriousness to reflect her class of elites and the privileged in the community.

Her adornment of the elaborate but simple geometrically patterned jewellery and decoration on the frills of her cloak (cover cloth) is an indication of her royal status and a membership of the elites and the privileged in the community. These enhance her nobility as elite. The presentation of the wind-flow draping at the right side of the composition expresses the fluidity and flexibility of *Dewurhen's* vocation which involves announcement and transmission of information from one destination to another in the community. As someone who has vocal and verbal prowess and potency, she possesses the ability to transfer and transmit the intentions and instructions of the unseen (spirit world) and the seen (leaders) to the community members.

The careful rendition of the folded pattern around the right arm creates an interlaced drapery below her right elbow. This echoes the cordial relationship that exists between the unseen and the seen, the elites (royals), the commoners and the wealthy (guilds and merchants). This therefore indicates that the thoughts and wisdom of chiefs (seen) represent that of the Unseen. In the Akan culture, the elites and chief will have to consult *Aberewa* (an unseen elderly woman) for direction and advice on matters that maybe contemptuous in nature. The folded pattern represents the support to the right arm – the arm that holds the throne and the gong-gong (the instrument that alerts and informs the community members of the intentions of the elite leaders).

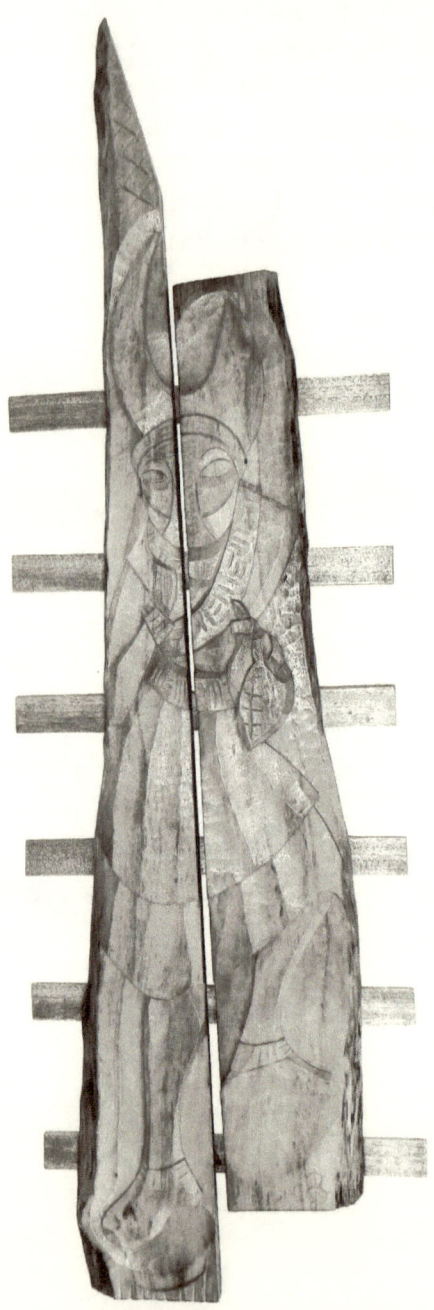

(PLATE: 9)
NKYERƐMBAHEN (FEMALE YOUTH CHIEF)
WOOD: NYAMKUM, DIMENSION: 193x51x5cm, YEAR 2013

NKYERƐMBAHEN (FEMALE YOUTH CHIEF)

Nkyerɛmbahen in the Akan culture literally represents the Female Youth Chief. It is a composition of a female figure playing music and dancing at the same time. This composition is produced from a two-piece irregular **Nyamkum** wood boards that have narrow parted-top portion, wider middle portion and a half-drop lower portion. Both boards are joined together vertically and have their sides display jagged edge with tree bark and sap. The source of the wood board can be traced to the small-scale wood market where it has been selected as wood fuel for food production. The top portion has linear pattern produced from V-gouge cuts. Both boards have a centimetre gab running through them vertically. They are supported at the back with six horizontal battens made from *Dahoma* wood.

Nkyerɛmbahen also known as **Nkatesiahen** wears a head gear made from horns and gold band. She also adorns herself with gold ornament, placed across her chest and around the head, neck, wrists and ankles. She wears the traditional mask-like face that is synonymous with Akan fertility dolls *(Ekuaba)*. The area stretching from the fore head across the nose down the mouth section is covered with a soft mesh.

Nkyerɛmbahen holds in her right hand *Afirikyiwa* a musical instrument played between the fingers. She is in a dancing posture with her right leg raised in readiness to step into the next pose. She wears a raffia skirt associated with spirituality and fertility.

Nkyerɛmbahen is an elected position that is conferred on a youth with visionary and achievable qualities. In addition, she must be someone who has the leadership and can-do spirit. She must be someone the community respects, adores and sees as possible and potent leader of the youth in the community at large. She must also be someone who is respectful, has good looks and who could be heard by the leaders (Chiefs) as an advocate of the youth in the community.

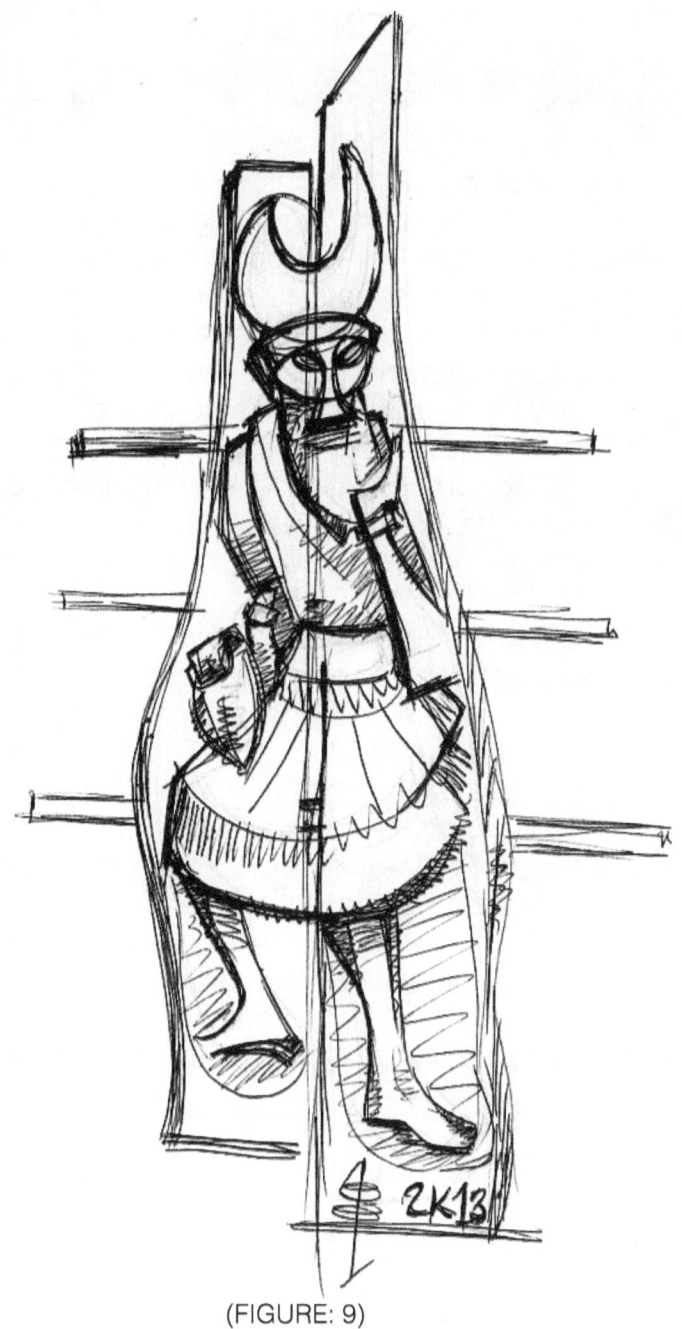

(FIGURE: 9)
NKYERᵋMBAHEN **(FEMALE YOUTH CHIEF)**

CONCEPT

Nkyerɛmbahen, a conveyor of thoughts and opinions of the people and who bears the concerns of the youth to and through the repositories of the customs and traditions of the community and to the ancestors, benevolent spirits, deities and Almighty God. Through her position as advocate of the youth, the community leaders through their good hearing capabilities are able to provide the needs and aspirations of the youth. This in effect promotes peace and development in the community. It is evident that among the Akan ethnic group, the youth constitute a greater proportion of the population. They are the driving force of the community's progress and prosperity. The youth are therefore the future human stock who will emerge as the future leaders of the community.

Nkyerɛmbahen wears on her head a pair of horns made from the bull. This object is often patronized by Akans. The bull is an animal that possesses enormous strength and might. Its horns are power symbols of chiefdom. This therefore echoes the quest for might by the royal. In fact, it is the beacon of hope that breeds progress and prosperity to satisfy human needs and capacity. Traditionally, as the conveyor of the thoughts and opinions of the youth, she is bound to appear noble and calm before her audiences and the community. *Nkyerɛmbahen* puts on a look which depicts half-closed eyes that bulge out of her sockets. Her face expresses a solemn facial looks that connotes that of the elites or the privileged in the community.

The wearing of the elaborate, but simple geometrically patterned jewellery and decoration at the fringes of her crown is an indication of her royal status, a member of the elites and the privileged society in the community. These append her nobility as an elite. The presentation of the mesh across the face and over the nose and mouth in the composition

67

expresses the ability to sift unpleasant utterances and offer wise and thoughtful words that may move communication beyond mere speeches to actions. The flexibility of her position as advocate of the youth requires her to transmit her thoughts and information in clear terms without ambiguity. As someone who has vocal and verbal prowess and potency, she possesses the ability to inform community leaders and elders the intentions and instructions of the unseen (spirits) and the seen (leaders) to the community members. This function may include the revelation of the aspirations the youth in the community.

The six horizontal battens made from *Dahoma* wood represents her quest to provide for all humanity irrespective of their background and lineage. *Dahoma* wood is that type of tough material that has the ability to resist termite and insect infestation. *Dahoma* can stay long in the soil as a building member. Likewise, it is a good material member for roof construction. This therefore reflects *Nkyerɛmbahen* position to pervade all odds to the benefit of her community. *Nkyerɛmbahen's* role as the youth leader of her community cannot be over looked and ignored. She is a force to reckon with in terms of her community's progress and peace.

The gold ornament that gilds *Nkyerɛmbahen* is a leap of adornment into her new role as the elites of the community. In the Akan culture, gold, a precious mineral, symbolizes royal status and state of honour and recognition. Gold is actually adorned by very important personalities for special occasions. On this account, its inclusion in Akan traditional apparel signifies prestige and honour. The careful rendition of the strand-patterned skirt fixed around the waist area creates an interspaced linear and flat drapery. This presents the cordial relationship that exists between the community authorities (the elite and royal), the youth, the older generation and the younger folks. This relationship is bound by the spiritual strength that surrounds chieftancy and community development.

Nkyerɛmbahen holds in the right hand 'Afirikyiwa' a ferrous metal shell-like musical instrument held and played within the fingers. The right hand is that of the human body that relates with spiritual matters. In the Akan culture, the left arm has a negative connotation and for that matter, it is not employed in the salutation of elder and important persons. Therefore for tradition and custom purposes, it is very right for the Nkyerɛmbahen to engage the right hand for all official responsibilities, hence, the placement of the Afirikyiwa in the right hand. Ferrous metal as a material has some amount of spiritual relationship with the African setting. It is the very material that can take life and also offer sustenance to man. Ferrous metal which is used in the production of musical instrument has the capability of beckoning to the spirit world to partake in the activities of the living.

The composition depicts Nkyerɛmbahen with a raised right foot. Like the right hand holding the musical instrument, the raised right foot has the responsibility of offering respect and honour to the elderly and the spirit world. This right foot is raised in an attempt to leap into the future and the unknown. The foot is an attempt to address some of the needs and demands of the generation present and unborn. There is an Akan adage that states that "sɛ igyina fakor a nna igyina w'adze do," literally meaning if you do not take a step towards solving an issue then nothing will be solved.

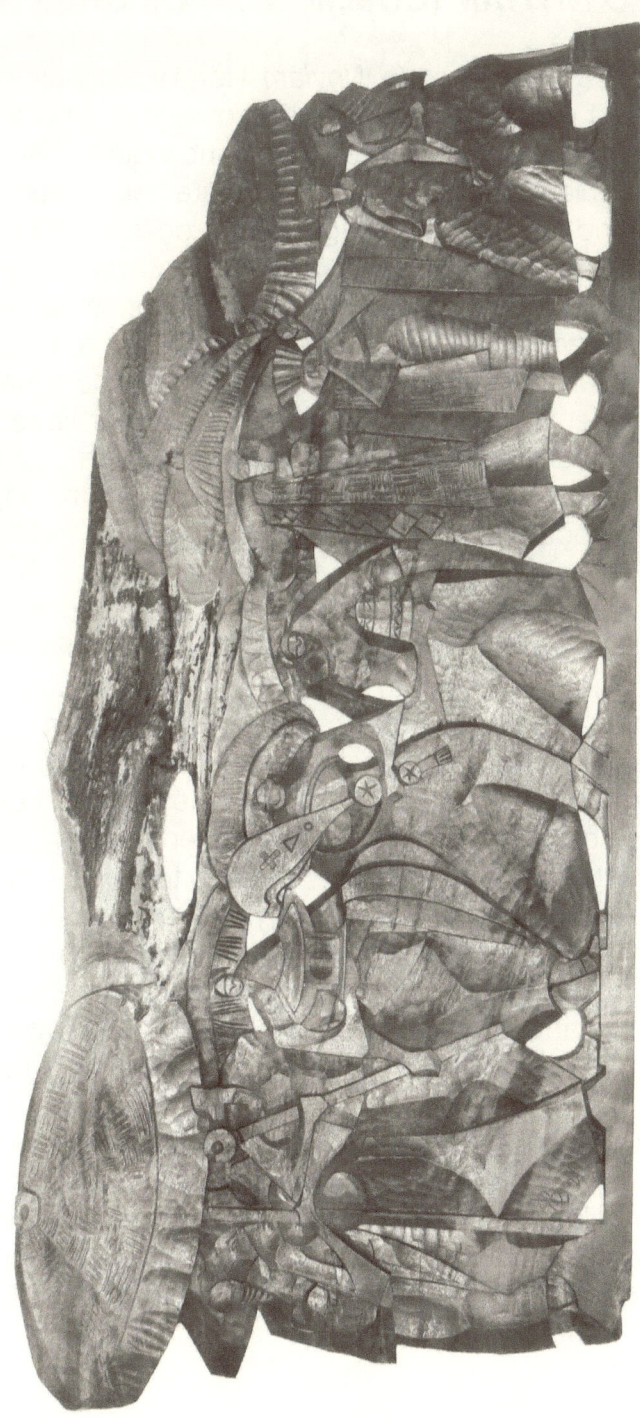

(PLATE: 10)
AHEMFO NHYIAM **(COMMUNION OF CHIEFS)**
WOOD: MAHOGANY, DIMENSION 165x80x3cm, YEAR 2002

AHEMFO NHYIAM (COMMUNION OF CHIEFS)

In the Akan culture, *Ahemfo Nhyiam* literally connotes the assemblage or convergence of chiefs of higher and lower ranks for the good of the community and individuals. Among the Akans, regular meetings of this nature are held to seek the intervention and the glory of Almighty God, deities, ancestors and other benevolent spirits. The composition was produced from a Mahogany board that is made up of a horizontal base-line and three irregular edges. The source of the mahogany wood board can be traced to the small-scale wood market where it has been selected as wood for domestic furniture production. The board showcases a crumpled top portion and a natural oval perforation that is made possible from the sap of the Mahogany board.

Additional, man-made perforations are created around the upper and the lower arms to provide a kind of artificial mesh and a see-through impression that allows colour, texture and images from the background to appear when the art piece hangs in position. The figures that are seen in this composition are rendered with certain aesthetic qualities; small heads, long necks, broader shoulders, elongated upper limbs, enlarged-shorter big legs and feet. Legs to these figures are either stretched or closed-up. The figures registered in this composition are rendered in simplified realism and has plain and angular cut pattern. Very little decorations are put on these figures and forms. *Ahemfo Nhyiam* displays the elites-sub-chiefs to the paramount chief in a left to right roll.

The trail of these sub-chiefs starts with *Edzebanhen*, the chief of welfare responsible for banquette, food energy and food safety. She holds a ceremonial pot that contains food, water and pleasurable drinks required to provide the paramount chief the needed food energy and pleasure. *Kyimhen* or *Bam-kyimhen* or *Akatadohen* – the chief of umbrella holds the handle of the umbrella. The canopy of the umbrella has been opened wide to provide shade and comfort to the chief. It also protects the chief from the harsh sunny weather. *Kyim-hen* is followed keenly by Akyeamehen. Akyeamehen, the chief of linguists, serves as the spokesman to the paramount chief when she sits in state. *Akyeamehen* bears the community mace that serves as the symbol of her office. *Eguahen*, the chief of stools, appears next in the composition. She holds the traditional stool, *Asɛsɛgua*, (a chair on which the chief sits when in state). This is the chair that contains the soul and being of the paramountcy. In the Akan culture, chiefs who do not possess stools are disregarded. Next in the trail is the *Afonahen* or *Akɔmfonahen*. She holds an exaggerated state sword, a symbolic war weapon that is representative of the authority and power of her office.

Egudzehen is positioned next to the *Afonahen*. *Egudzehen* is the chief in charge of jewellery and ornament for the para-mount chief. She holds an elaborate jewellery pot across her torso. This jewellery pot is also the symbol of her office. Tamhen, the chief of cloth comes next in the trail after the *Egudzehen*. She is presented with a traditional designer cloth which is meant to embellish the chief who is also the symbolic icon of her state. The exhibited cloths drip down from her shoulder and her arms.

Abɔtsirhen, chief of head crown and head bands appears next in the royal trail. She carries a head crown decorated with the horn and the feathers. *Abɔtsirhen*, is followed closely by the *Akɔmfohen*-chief of the traditional priests of the para-mountcy. *Akɔmfohen* is also known as *Akɔmhen*. She is responsible for the spiritual security and religious upliftment of the paramouncy as well as the state. She takes care of the entire spiritual growth of the chiefdom and community. She holds in her hand whisks – tail furs of lion and horse. These whisks serve as the symbol of her office.

At the extreme right stands the *Papaahen* which literally means chief of fan. She holds a large fan across her chest. In the Akan chiefdom culture, when chiefs are in-state or in royal trail, they are constantly fanned to make them comfortable. Akan chiefs are noted for putting on apparel and ornament that generate some amount of heat. Also, when there is a durbar and a lot of persons converge, there is normally a lot of heat generated. Hence, the Papaahen's role becomes indispensable under such circumstances.

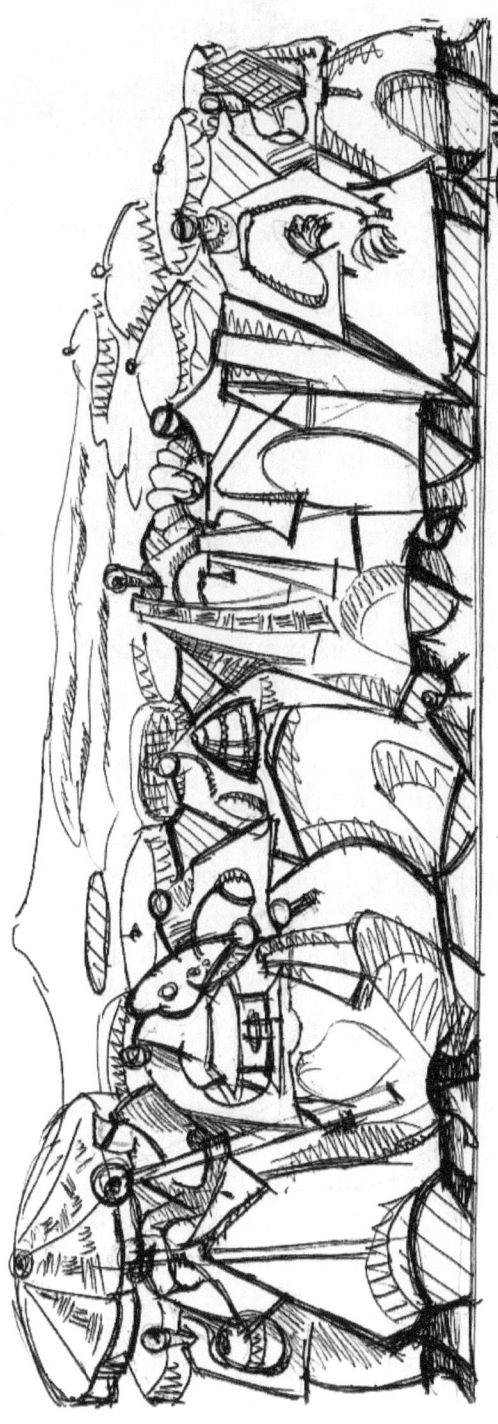

(FIGURE: 10)
AHEMFO NHYIAM (COMMUNION OF CHIEFS)

CONCEPT

In the Akan culture, sub-chiefs are elected to perform several roles on behalf of the paramount chief and the community. They are therefore supposed to support the paramount chief to function well since the paramount chief cannot be everywhere at all times to perform all necessary functions. The sub-chiefs can therefore be likened to ministerial rankings in the Western governance system. There is the adage that *Ɔmanhen a onyi aboafo nndzi mu'* literally means a paramount chief without sub-chiefs has no paramountcy. In effect, the sub-chiefs found in the **Ahemfo Nhyiam** composition have the due responsibility of ensuring the health, spiritual, social, political, entertainment, and well being of the paramount chief and the community alike.

The upper section of this composition showcases a crumpled burnt umber and pale yellow sap with an oval perforation positioned within. The burnt umber crumpled form and the natural oval perforation are symbolically associated with night and day. The burnt umber represents the night which connotes spirituality, natural challenges, nefarious acts, mishaps. It also represents the symbol of hope for the future. Again, the burnt umber signifies the unseen world where certain spiritual activities happen without human intervention and understanding. The crumpled nature of the wood board reflects the movement of the clouds which is an activity of nature is beyond human comprehension. These clouds, therefore, predict the unseen, the mystery as well as the hope for a better future. Similarly, the presence of the oval shape perforated through the wood board signifies the appearance of the sun and moon. The sun and the moon are part of natural occurrences that bring to humanity the light for hope, prosperity, progress and development. The sun and the moon have the power to overcome the activity of the night. This, in effect, brings to mankind hope, prosperity and development. Therefore, the success of the chiefdom, the state and the community depends largely on the interplay of the activities of night and day. The perforations around the upper and lower arms of the sub-chiefs mirror the symbolism of the sun towards humanity. Therefore, all sub-chiefs have to strive to shine in their elected office. This will eventually bring progress and development to the paramountcy and the community.

The large circular umbrella at the extreme top left of the composition symbolizes the presence and dominance of the paramountcy over the sub-chiefs. The small-sized and medium-sized umbrella represents the sub-chiefs. This large umbrella is linked to the numerous smaller umbrellas. This reveals the relationship that exists between the paramount chief and the sub-chiefs. The sub-chiefs in this composition are represented with smaller heads. They are sub-chiefs to the paramount chief (Ɔ*manhen*). They are subservient to the Ɔ*manhen* whose is presumed to be bigger but absent in the composition. This reflects smaller head for smaller umbrellas and the larger head for the larger umbrellas.

The sub-chiefs rendered in the composition are projected as having a firm, solid figure. They have elongated upper limbs and shorter, but enlarged lower limbs and also feet that can be likened to elephants and lion legs and feet. They are large and stable just for the betterment of the Akan chiefdom. This is evident of the stability and strength that exists within and among these lesser ranked chiefs. This, therefore, projects the support base that the paramountcy requires of the elites and the community.

The firm and solid necks to the figures are synonymous with the strength in the neck of a tiger, the task of the elephant and the neck of Giraffe. These power-animals have the capacity to hold and grip firmly. They, therefore, provide the culture of chiefdom, the support and direction to determine the paramountcy and the community's preferences. All these supports are necessary and essential because the supremacy of the paramountcy and that of the state and communities must be successful.

The principle based on same status, equal responsibility and equal rights reflects the presence of the horizontal nature of the board's baseline. This baseline places all sub-chiefs at the same level of recognition and responsibility. These sub-chiefs are therefore expected to experience communion of strength, ideas and support towards the success of the paramountcy and the community. Therefore the over-simplification of the apparel put on by the sub-chiefs as well as the absence of elaborate ornamentation on the sub-chiefs presents a manifestation of their subservient responsibility and allegiance towards the paramount chief - *Ɔmanhen*.

In effect, it is imperative that Chiefdom among the Akans, respects ranks, order, authority and responsibility. Therefore, all sub-chiefs are elected to see to the well being and success of the paramountcy, their state and their community.

REFERENCES

• Kottak, Conrad Phillip. (1973). Band. Cultural Anthropology. Vol. 14. New York: McGraw HIll, 2011.

• Erdal, D. & Whiten, A. (1996) "Egalitarianism and Machiavellian Intelligence in Human Evolution" in Mellars, (15 June 2013 at 15:30).

• P. & Gibson, K. (eds) Modelling the Early Human Mind. Cambridge Macdonald Monograph Series. (15 June 2013 at 15:30)

• Chiefdom, From http://www.Wikipedia, the free encyclopaedia (15 June 2013 at 16:30)

• http://www.Britannica encyclopaedia. (15 June 2013 at 17:30)

• Robert L. Carneiro: (1981) "An autonomous political unit comprising a number of villages or communities under the permanent control of a paramount chief" (Carneiro 1981: 45).

• Oil-City Magazine, (2003) Chieftancy, Takoradi Ghana.

• 1992 Constitution of Ghana, Chapter 22, Section 270(1)

• APPIAH E.R.K. (1999) General Knowledge in Arts, Accra, Ghana

• BENTUM, S.A. (2013) Aesthetics and Appreciation of Tree Trunks and Branches into sketches and Sculptures, Trafford Inc. USA/Canada.

• Country Review Report and Programme of Action of the

Republic of Ghana, Africa Peer Review Mechanism
(2005:142)

• Otumfo Osei Tutu, King of the Asantis, fifteenth years of
enstoolment, anniversary address United Television (UTV)
Afternoon News (11 May 2014)

• Burkes Peerage: See Irish and Scottish Chiefs; Peerages;
and Titles

• Ellis, Peter Berresford, Erin's Blood Royal: The Gaelic
Noble Dynasties of Ireland. Palgrave. Revised edition, 2002.

• Murphy, Sean J (2004) Twilight of the Chiefs: The Mac
Carthy Mór Hoax. Bethesda, Maryland: Academica Press.
ISBN 1-930901-43-7.

• MacLysaght, Edward (1996) More Irish Families. Dublin,
Ireland: Irish Academic Press. ISBN 0-7165-2604-2.

• Nicholls, K.W. Gaelic and Gaelicized Ireland in the Middle
Ages Dublin, Lilliput Press, 2003. ISBN 1-84351-003-0.

• Vanishing Kingdoms - The Irish Chiefs and Their Families,
by Walter J. P. Curley (former US Ambassador to Ireland),
with foreword by Charles Lysaght, published by The Lilliput
Press, Dublin, 2004. ISBN 1-84351-055-3 & ISBN
1-84351-056-1. (Chapter on O'Donnell of Tyrconnell, page
59).

• Nash, Professor C., Of Irish Descent, chapter 4. New York,
Syracuse University Press, 2008. ISBN 978-0-8156-3159-0
• http://www.behaviorresearch.net/presentations.htm Title;

• Godwin Sogolo, (1993) Foundations of African Philosophy,
A Definitive Analysis of Conceptual Issues in   African

Thought, Publisher; Ibadan University Press, Place; Ibadan, Nigeria.

• William Wheeler & Charles H. Hayward, 1979 Wood Carving, Duke Publication, Sterling Publishing Company, New York

• Ghana Hardwoods

www.ingramcontent.com/pod-product-compliance
Lightning Source LLC
Chambersburg PA
CBHW030916180526
45163CB00004B/1857